MORE

MIDDLE SCHOOL
TALKSHEETS

EPIC OLD TESTAMENT STORIES

FOR AGES 11-14

52 READY-TO-USE DISCUSSIONS

DAVID LYNN

 youth specialties

 ZONDERVAN®

ZONDERVAN.com/
AUTHORTRACKER
follow your favorite authors

ZONDERVAN

More Middle School TalkSheets, Epic Old Testament Stories
Copyright © 2012 by David Lynn

Requests for information should be addressed to:

Zondervan, Grand Rapids, Michigan 49530

ISBN 978-0-310-88932-8

Cover design: Tammy Johnson
Interior design: David Conn

Printed in the United States of America

12   13   14   15   16   /DCI/   20   19   18   17   16   15   14   13   12   11   10   9   8   7   6   5   4   3   2   1

CONTENTS

THE HOWS AND WHATS OF OLD TESTAMENT TALKSHEETS

You are holding a very valuable book! No, it won't make you a genius or millionaire, but it does contain a year's worth of instant discussions to help middle school youth develop as disciples. Inside you'll find reproducible OLD TESTAMENT Talk-Sheets that cover 52 stories from the judges to Josiah finding God's Word—plus simple, step-by-step instructions on how to use them. All you need is this book, a few copies of the handouts, some young people (and maybe a snack or two), and you're on your way to landing on some serious issues in teenagers' lives.

These OLD TESTAMENT TalkSheets are user-friendly and very flexible. You can use them in a youth group meeting, a Sunday school class, or a Bible study group. You can adapt them for either large or small groups. And you can cover the material in as little as 20 minutes or explore it more intensively over two hours.

You can build an entire youth group meeting around a single OLD TESTAMENT TalkSheet, or you can use OLD TESTAMENT TalkSheets to supplement your other materials and resources. These TalkSheets are tools for you—but how you use them is up to you.

More Middle School OLD TESTAMENT TalkSheets is not your average curriculum or workbook. This collection of discussions will get your young people involved and excited about talking through important issues. The OLD TESTAMENT TalkSheets deal with epic stories and include interesting activi-

ties, challenging talks, and thought-provoking questions. They'll get your youth forming new opinions, learning about themselves, and growing in their faith.

IMPORTANT GUIDING PRINCIPLES BEFORE USING OLD TESTAMENT TALKSHEETS

Let's begin by agreeing on two primary principles:

1. Faith is essentially caught not taught, and
2. The Holy Spirit alone works best to establish faith within teenagers' lives, changing them from knowers to believers, from church attendees to lifelong followers of Jesus.

If we can agree on these two principles, then it's easier to explain how *More OLD TESTAMENT TalkSheets* is designed. It's not so much a teaching tool as a tool designed to engage real faith connections and encourage faith vocabulary in young people's lives.

So many church attendees don't know how to articulate their faith, nor do they often perceive vital connections to their faith outside the church building. Which is why OLD TESTAMENT Talk-Sheets' exercises are designed to help young people connect what they believe to their day-to-day lives, as well as develop a living faith vocabulary as opposed to a church vocabulary used only during church to please adults and religious leaders. For faith to grow with us, throughout our lives, we must discover faith's vital connection in "real time." To see how and where Jesus in our lives engages the real world. And we must express this connection through a "vocabulary of faith" that grows with us and goes with us, as opposed to expressing "church language" we reserve for religious settings and certain occasions.

Our Lord Jesus used the concept of fishing to connect his first followers with what he was doing, using words and images that were familiar to them. In the same way, you can use these OLD TESTAMENT TalkSheets to create settings in which young people can talk about faith, employing familiar concepts that help develop faith vocabulary and deepen faith by connecting it to relevant life experiences.

OLD TESTAMENT TalkSheets as an Engaging Tool More Than a Teaching Tool

I believe we've often made a very fundamental mistake in how we assist young people in developing their faith: We've hammered down on obvious answers to questions that they're often not even asking. And as a result youth can answer questions "correctly" but don't see why the answers are relevant to their daily lives.

Take for example the primary question of faith: *Who is your Lord and Savior?* The right answer, of course, is "Jesus Christ is my Lord and Savior." I've heard young people answer this question correctly for many years. But I've also witnessed many young people get stumped regarding what *Lord* means in a culture in which we're all our own sources of truth, or why we need to be saved when everyone is basically okay. We mistakenly believe that just having good information is enough. But the information needs vitality and relevance that youth can wrestle with.

This is why we believe that young people must understand the tensions of life from which questions arise and struggle with how to answer those questions before they hear how God addresses lordship and salvation in the person of Jesus Christ. Then we can ask, "If this is how life is, then who is YOUR Lord and Savior?"

By engaging young people inwardly—"INNER-gizing" them into a real dialogue about their lives, their perceptions, and their faith—we can create pathways upon which we can partner with them as they grow as disciples.

A Common Pitfall to Avoid

Faith development is often a multi-step process. Some things must be set in place before other things can be embraced. For example, we might say a person moves from A to B before moving on to C and eventually arriving at D; but many leaders mistakenly view the move from A to D as a simple task and grow impatient for those under their care to make that developmental leap. And people may be willing to make leaps they're not ready for because they trust their leaders or are afraid to express doubts in "unsafe" environments. They also may believe they lack faith and feel guilty. And sometimes people just want to fit in.

I've witnessed these conditions where real faith isn't deep enough to sustain the pressures of real life, and substitutional faith is worn like a garment in God's house. Such followers attend gatherings but cannot pray for themselves, hold a secret doubt and guilt, and often defer to leaders on all matters of faith. Jesus says such followers are like shallow soil on which the seed falls and eventually dies.

Instead good Christian leaders understand that they're guides on the roadside as people follow the Master.

Essentially a discussion leader can fill three roles: a Tool, a Thorn, or a Stage Director:

- Tool: A force in the hand of the Holy Spirit that works in a young person's life during the process of faith building.
- Thorn: The leader becomes an irritant in disciples' lives, which can alienate them from the faith community due to the unsafe faith environment and unrealistic expectations and impatient discipleship methods.
- Stage Director: Leader inoculates young people against "catching" real faith by creating an environment that encourages wearing masks of belief and speaking a kind of church language, effectively insulating them from

embracing a real, vital faith expressed in a living language.

Clearly only one role serves well here: the Tool.

OLD TESTAMENT TalkSheets Can Help Us Be Good Stewards of a Sacred Process

But if we understand that deep, rich soil may take time and much mulching if a seed is to take root, then we can as leaders trust that faith is not about us achieving something in others' lives but about the Holy Spirit shaping followers' lives. We can become stewards of a most sacred process. Young people can pick up useless notions of faith and life on their way to discovering real faith through vital discipleship, and if these useless notions are to be replaced with life-giving awareness in a living, vital faith in Jesus, we must offer patience and loving mentoring.

Remember that Thomas didn't at first believe that Jesus was resurrected even though the other disciples expressed to him what they had witnessed. It's a great testimony of those early followers of Jesus that Thomas was still with them "in their midst" a week later when Jesus showed up and confirmed himself to Thomas. In the same way it's important to create a safe environment where youth can explore their faith and express themselves without the expectation of correct performance or the pressure to make a developmental leap that they're not ready to sustain as a disciple until, for them, Jesus shows up.

LEADING AN OLD TESTAMENT TALKSHEET DISCUSSION

OLD TESTAMENT TalkSheets can be used as a curriculum for your youth group, but they're designed as discussion springboards. They encourage your young people to take part and interact with each other while talking about real-life issues. And hopefully they'll do some serious thinking, discover new ideas for themselves, defend their points of view, and make decisions.

Youth today face a world of moral confusion. Teenagers are bombarded with the voices of society and the media—most of which drown out what they hear from the church. Youth leaders must teach the church's beliefs and values—and also help young people make right choices in a world full of options.

An OLD TESTAMENT TalkSheet discussion works to remedy this. While dealing with the questions and activities on the OLD TESTAMENT TalkSheet, your young people will think carefully about issues, compare their beliefs and values with others, and make their own choices. OLD TESTAMENT TalkSheets also will challenge your youth to explain and rework their ideas in a Christian atmosphere of acceptance, support, and growth.

One of the most common fears among middle school youth group leaders is, "What will I do if the young people in my group just sit there and don't say anything?" Well, when young people don't have anything to say, it's because they haven't had a chance or time to get their thoughts organized! Most young people haven't developed the ability to think on their feet. Since many are afraid they might sound stupid, they don't even attempt to figure out how to voice their ideas and opinions.

Again, OLD TESTAMENT TalkSheets let your youth deal with the issues in a challenging, non-threatening way before the actual discussion begins. They'll have time to organize their thoughts, write them down, and ease their fears about participating. They may even look forward to sharing their answers! Most importantly, they'll want to find out what others said and open up to talk through the topics.

If you're still a little leery about the success of a real discussion among your youth, that's okay! The only way to get them rolling is to get them started.

Your Role as the Leader

The best discussions don't happen by accident. They require careful preparation and a sensitive leader. Don't worry if you aren't experienced or don't have hours to prepare. OLD TESTAMENT Talk-Sheets are designed to help even the novice leader! The more OLD TESTAMENT TalkSheet discussions you lead, the easier it becomes. Keep the following tips in mind when using the OLD TESTAMENT TalkSheets as you get your young people talking.

Be Choosy

Each OLD TESTAMENT TalkSheet deals with a different story. Under the title of each OLD TESTAMENT TalkSheet is a subtitle expressing its theme; you can use the subtitle to choose an OLD TESTAMENT Talk-Sheet to match your group's needs and maturity level. Don't feel obligated to use the OLD TESTA-MENT TalkSheets in the order they appear in this book, either. Use your best judgment and mix them up however you want—they are tools for you!

Make Copies

Each student will need a copy of the TalkSheet—which is the right-facing page. The material on the reverse side (the Leader's Guide) is just for you. You can make copies for your group only—but *not* every group in your town!—because we've given you permission to do so. But U.S. copyright laws have not changed, and it's still mandatory to request permission from a publisher before making copies of other published material. Thank you for cooperating.

Try It Yourself

Once you've chosen an OLD TESTAMENT TalkSheet for your group, answer the questions and do the activities yourself. Imagine your young people's reactions to the OLD TESTAMENT TalkSheet. This will help you prepare for the discussion and understand what you're asking them to do. Plus you'll have some time to think of other appropriate questions, activities, and Bible verses.

Get Some Insight

On each Leader's Guide page you'll find numerous tips and ideas for getting the most out of your discussion. You may want to add some of your own thoughts or ideas in the margins.

Set Up for the Talk

Make sure the seating arrangement is inclusive and encourages a comfortable, safe atmosphere for discussion. Theater-style seating (in rows) isn't discussion-friendly; instead arrange the chairs in a circle or semicircle (or on the floor with pillows!).

Introduce the Topic

You may introduce the topic before you pass out the OLD TESTAMENT TalkSheets to your group and then allow the topic to develop as you use the material. We have a simple format on the Leader's Guide that can help your introduction: In the "Read Out Loud" section, simply read the paragraph/s aloud, and then ask a young person to read the story from the Bible. After the story is read, you can use the question in the "Ask" section to get the group primed for a discussion of the story.

Depending on your group, keep your introduction short and to the point. Be careful not to over-introduce the topic, sound preachy, or resolve the issue before you've started. Your goal is to spark their interest and leave plenty of room for discussion, allowing the material to introduce the topic.

Now you're on your way! The following are excellent methods you can use to introduce any topic in this book—

- Show a related short film or video.
- Read a passage from a book or magazine that relates to the subject.
- Play a popular CD/DVD that deals with the topic.
- Perform a short skit or dramatic presentation.
- Play a simulation game or role-play, setting up the topic.

- Present current statistics, survey results, or read a newspaper article that provides recent information about the topic.
- Use an icebreaker or other crowd game, getting into the topic in a humorous way.
- Use posters, videos, or other visuals to help focus attention on the topic.

There are endless possibilities for an intro—you are limited only by your own creativity! Keep in mind that a clear, simple introduction is a very important part of each session.

Set Boundaries

It'll be helpful to set a few ground rules before the discussion. Keep the rules to a minimum, of course, but let youth know what's expected of them. The following are suggestions for some basic ground rules:

- **What's said in this room stays in this room.** Emphasize the importance of confidentiality. Some young people will open up easier than others, but if your youth can't keep the discussion in the room, then no one will open up.
- **No put-downs.** Mutual respect is important. If your young people disagree with some opinions, ask them to comment on the subject (not who made the comment). It's okay to attack the ideas, but not the people behind them.
- **There's no such thing as a dumb question.** Your group members must feel free to ask questions at any time. The best way to learn is to ask questions and get answers.
- **No one is forced to talk.** Let everyone know they have the right to pass or not answer any question.
- **Only one person speaks at a time.** This is a mutual respect issue, too. Everyone's opinion is worthwhile and deserves to be heard without competing voices.

Communicate with your group that everyone needs to respect these boundaries. If you sense that your group members are attacking each other or behaving otherwise negatively during the discussion, stop and deal with the problem before going on.

Allow Enough Time

Pass out copies of the OLD TESTAMENT TalkSheet to your young people after the introduction and make sure that each person has a pen or pencil and a Bible. There are usually five or six activities on each OLD TESTAMENT TalkSheet. If your time is limited, or if you're using only a part of the OLD TESTAMENT TalkSheet, tell the group to complete only the activities you'd like them to complete.

Decide ahead of time if you'd like them to work on the OLD TESTAMENT TalkSheets individually or in groups.

Let them know how much time they have to complete the OLD TESTAMENT TalkSheet and when there's a minute (or so) left. Start the discussion when everyone seems ready to go.

Set the Stage

Create a climate of acceptance. Most teenagers are afraid to voice their opinions because they don't want to be laughed at or look stupid in front of their peers. They want to feel safe when it comes to sharing their feelings and beliefs. Communicate that they can share their thoughts and ideas—even if they may be different or unpopular. If they hear put-downs, criticism, laughter, or snide remarks (even if their statements are opposed to the Bible) directed at them, it'll hurt the discussion.

Always phrase your questions so that you're asking for an opinion, not an answer. For example, "What should Bill have done in that situation?" should be rephrased with the simple addition of three words: "What *do you think* Bill should have done in that situation?" That makes the question more of an opinion and, therefore, less threatening;

you're not after them for the "right" answer. Your young people will relax when they feel more comfortable and confident. Plus, they'll know you actually care about their opinions, and they'll feel appreciated!

Lead the Discussion

Discuss the OLD TESTAMENT TalkSheet with the group and encourage all your young people to participate. Communicate that it's important for them to respect each other's opinions and feelings! The more they contribute, the better the discussion will be.

If your youth group is big, you may divide it into smaller groups of six to 12. Each of these small groups should have a facilitator—either an adult leader or a mature teen leader—to keep the discussion going. Remind the facilitators to not dominate the discussion. In fact, instruct facilitators to redirect questions or responses to the group if they keep looking to leaders for answers. Once the smaller groups have completed their discussions, combine them into one large group and ask the different groups to share their ideas.

Hint: You don't have to divide the groups up with every OLD TESTAMENT TalkSheet. For some discussions, you may want to vary the group size or divide the meeting into groups of the same sex.

The discussion should target the questions and answers on the OLD TESTAMENT TalkSheet. Go through them one at a time and ask the young people to share their responses. Have them compare their answers and brainstorm new ones in addition to the ones they've written down. Encourage them to share their opinions and answers, but don't force responses from those who are quiet.

Affirm All Responses, Right or Wrong

Let your young people know that their comments and contributions are appreciated and important. This is especially true for those who rarely speak up—make a point of thanking them for joining in.

This will be an incentive for them to participate further in future sessions.

Remember, though, that affirmation doesn't mean approval. Affirm even those comments that seem wrong to you. You'll show that everyone has a right to express their ideas, no matter how controversial. If someone states an opinion that's off base, make a mental note of the comment. Then in your wrap-up, come back to the comment or present a different point of view in a positive way. But *don't* reprimand the person who voiced the comment.

Don't Be the Answer Authority

Some young people believe you, as a leader, have the correct answer to every question. They'll look to you for approval. If they start to focus on you for answers or approval that they're "correct," redirect them toward the group by saying something like, "Remember that you're talking to everyone, not just me."

Your goal as the facilitator is to keep the discussion alive and kicking. It's important that your young people think of you as a member of the group—on their level. The less authoritative you are, the more value your opinions will carry. If your young people view you as a peer, they will listen to your comments more openly. You have a tremendous responsibility to be, with sincerity, their trusted friend.

Listen to Each Person

God gave you one mouth and two ears. Good discussion leaders know how to listen. Encourage others to talk first—then express your opinions during your wrap-up.

Don't Force It

Encourage all your young people to talk, but don't require them to comment. Each member has the right to pass. If you don't believe the discussion is going well, move to the next question or restate the question to keep things going.

Don't Take Sides

Be extra careful not to take one side over another. Instead encourage both sides to think through and even talk through their positions—ask questions to get them going deeper. If everyone agrees on an issue, you can play devil's advocate with tough questions and stretch their thinking. Remain as neutral as possible.

Don't Let Anyone (Including You) Take Over

Nearly every youth group has one person who likes to talk and is perfectly willing to express an opinion on any subject, all the time. Try to encourage equal participation from all the young people.

Let Them Laugh!

Discussions can be fun! Most of the OLD TESTAMENT TalkSheets include questions that'll elicit laughter and get youth thinking, too.

Let Them Be Silent

Silence can be scary for discussion leaders! Some react by trying to fill the silence with a question or comment. The following suggestions may help you to handle silence more effectively:

- *Get comfortable with silence.* Wait for 30 seconds or so to respond. You may want to restate the question to give your young people a gentle nudge.
- *Talk about the silence with the group.* What does the silence mean? Do they really not have any comments? Maybe they're confused, embarrassed, or don't want to share.
- *If you acknowledge the silence, it may break the ice.* Answer the silence with questions or comments such as, "I know this is challenging to think about . . ." or "It's scary to be the first to talk."
- *Ask a different question that may be easier to handle.* Or at least one that will clarify the one already posed. But don't do this too quickly,

without giving them time to think the first one through.

Keep It Under Control

Monitor the discussion. Be aware if it's going in a certain direction or off track. This can happen quickly, especially if there's disagreement or things get heated. Mediate wisely and set the tone you want. If your group gets bored with an issue, get things back on track. Let the discussion unfold but be sensitive to who is/isn't getting involved.

If a young person brings up an interesting side issue, decide whether or not to pursue it. If discussion is going well and the issue is worth it, let them talk it through. But if things get way off track, you might say something like, "Let's come back to that subject later if we have time. Right now, let's finish our discussion on . . ."

Be Creative and Flexible

You don't have to follow the order of the questions on the OLD TESTAMENT TalkSheet. Follow your creative instinct. If you find other ways to use the OLD TESTAMENT TalkSheets, use them! Go ahead and add other questions or Bible references.

Don't feel pressured to spend time on every single activity, either. If you're short on time, skip some items. Stick with the questions that are the most interesting to the group.

Set Your Goals

OLD TESTAMENT TalkSheets are designed to move toward a goal, but you need to identify your goal in advance. What would you like your young people to learn? What truth should they discover? What's the goal of the session? If you don't know where you're going, it's doubtful you'll get there. As stated earlier, there's a theme for each of the OLD TESTAMENT TalkSheets. You'll find this theme under each of the TalkSheet titles on the contents page.

Be There for Your Young People

Some young people may want to talk more with you (you got 'em thinking!). Let them know that you can talk one-on-one with them afterward. Communicate that they can feel free to talk confidentially with you about anything. Let them know you're there for them with support and concern, even after the OLD TESTAMENT TalkSheet discussion has been completed.

Close the Discussion

OLD TESTAMENT TalkSheets work best with a strong concluding presentation. You can use "The Close" section at the end of each Leader's Guide for this. Present a challenge to the group by asking yourself, *What do I want my young people to remember most from this discussion?* There's your wrap-up!

Sometimes you won't even need a wrap-up. You may want to leave the issue hanging and discuss it during another meeting. That way your group can think more about the issue, and you can nail down the final ideas later.

A FINAL WORD TO THE WISE—THAT'S YOU!

Some of these OLD TESTAMENT TalkSheets deal with topics that may be sensitive or controversial for your young people. You're encouraging discussion and inviting them to express their opinions, and as a result parents or others in your church who don't see the importance of such discussions may criticize you. So use your best judgment. If you suspect that a particular OLD TESTAMENT TalkSheet will cause problems, you may want to skip it. Or you may want to tweak a particular OLD TESTAMENT TalkSheet and only cover some of the questions. Either way, the potential bad could outweigh the good—better safe than sorry. And to avoid any misunderstanding, you may want to give the parents or senior pastor (or the person to whom you're accountable) copies of the OLD TESTAMENT TalkSheet before you use it. Let them know the discussion you're planning and the goal you're hoping to accomplish. Challenge your young people to take their OLD TESTAMENT TalkSheets home to talk about it with their parents. *How would their parents, as young people, have answered the questions?* Your young people may find that their parents understand them better than they thought! Also, encourage them to think of other Bible verses or ways that the OLD TESTAMENT TalkSheet applies to their lives.

Barak Rocks (and So Does Deb)

Great things can be accomplished for God if we don't care who gets the credit

1. What do you do when you sin?

❏ I never tell God that I'm sorry.
❏ I sometimes tell God that I'm sorry.
❏ I usually tell God that I'm sorry.
❏ I always tell God that I'm sorry.

2. Who, like Deborah, is God's voice in your life?

❏ Mother or father
❏ Grandparent
❏ Pastor
❏ Adult friend
❏ Friends my age

3. The Canaanites tormented God's people, the Israelites, for 20 long years. The Israelites at times felt abandoned by God.

❏ I often feel like God has abandoned me.
❏ I sometimes feel like God has abandoned me.
❏ I hardly ever feel like God has abandoned me.
❏ I never feel like God has abandoned me.

4. Monica was not happy. She collected 25 cans of food from neighbors and family members for her church's food drive. She knew she brought more food to the drive than anyone else—but no one seemed to notice! Someone should at least say something about how much she cared for hungry people in her community.

What do you think of Monica's attitude?

5. Deborah and Barak saw God use them to defeat their enemies, the Canaanites. I would like to see God . . . (check all that apply)

❏ make me a nicer person at home.
❏ give me a suitcase full of money.
❏ change my teachers.
❏ punish my enemies.
❏ show up at my school.
❏ make my life easier.
❏ give me more trials.

READ OUT LOUD

God's people, the Israelites, have again returned to idolatry. They had been at peace for two generations—80 years. But now they had moved away from the worship of the Lord, instead turning to the false gods of the Canaanites, their neighbors. So the Lord allowed the Canaanites to invade and conquer the Israelites. The Canaanite King, Jabin, had assembled an incredible army with 900 chariots. This army, led by a guy named Sisera, could crush anyone or anything in its path. God's people were doomed. Or were they? Read about what happened in Judges 4:1-16.

ASK

Do you get the credit you deserve for the work you do at school?

DISCUSS, BY THE NUMBERS

1. God's people, the Israelites "did evil in the eyes of the Lord" (Judges 4:1) so God allowed their enemies, the Canaanites, to brutally torment them. After 20 years of this oppression, the Israelites finally repented of their sins and "cried to the Lord for help" (Judges 4:3). Ask, "How are we like the Israelites?" Explore with your group members why it takes so long for us to tell God we're sorry and want to change our behavior.

2. This may be a new concept for many of your group members. However, it is vitally important that they identify people in their lives who are strong followers of Christ; those who can speak God's Word and truth to them. This is not referring to a cult-like obedience to another human being; it's about having a circle of people around them who can help them identify what God is saying and how God is leading. Deborah was God's mouthpiece as both judge and prophet for the people of Israel. Search with your group for people in your congregation who can be God's voice in their lives.

3. Barak obeyed the Lord and assembled an army to fight the Canaanites. Remember, it seemed like God had abandoned Israel for 20 years, and yet Barak was faithful. Listen to the stories your group members tell of times they felt abandoned by God.

Tell a story of when you felt abandoned by the Lord. Discuss together the ways we practice realizing God's presence, especially when God feels far away—repentance, silence, prayer, Bible reading, worship, and fellowship.

4. Barak was willing to do exactly what God commanded without getting the credit. Use this situation to discuss with your group members today's idea—*Great things can be accomplished for God if we don't care who gets the credit.*

5. See commentary in bold after each statement:
   - make me a nicer person at home. **God will help you change your attitude and actions at home if you surrender your will to God's.**
   - give me a suitcase full of money. **God will provide for your basic needs, but God probably won't throw money at you.**
   - change my teachers. **God is in the business of changing you and the way you respond to your teachers.**
   - punish my enemies. **How about trying to love your enemies as Jesus tells us to do? Impossible as this may sound, God stands ready to do this *through you.***
   - show up at my school. **Look for God at your school. God has been there all along.**
   - make my life easier. **God may or may not do this. But God will walk through the tough times with you.**
   - give me more trials. **God will do what God thinks is best for your life.**

THE CLOSE

Barak and Deborah both teach us that great things can be accomplished for God if we don't care who gets the credit. Both of them surrendered their lives to God so that God could work in them and through them. God did not disappoint. God gave them an amazing victory. God can and will do the same in our lives if we only submit.

1. **Are your friends more like or less like Jephthah?**

    ❏ My friends are like Jephthah—they won't do anything for me unless there's something in it for them.
    ❏ My friends are not like Jephthah—they will do anything for me without expecting something in return.

Who Are You Becoming?

We imitate who (or what) we worship

2. **Jephthah was an outcast living among people who worshiped false gods. Instead of learning how big and loving God really is from those who believe, he learned from unbelievers about small and petty false gods like Chemosh and Molech.**

    What are you learning about Jesus from your congregation's worship time?
    What are you learning about Jesus from your youth group or small group?
    What are you learning about Jesus in your home?

3. **What or who you worship influences who you become. Underline the response in the parenthesis that best completes each statement.**

    When you worship money you become (rich, greedy, Christlike).
    When you worship alcohol you become (addicted, popular, Christlike).
    When you worship celebrities you become (important, shallow, Christlike).
    When you worship looks you become (good-looking, self-absorbed, Christlike).
    When you worship friends you become (insecure, a loser, Christlike).

4. **Jephthah lived with people who worshiped false gods that were viewed as smaller and weaker than the God of the Bible. What gods do your friends worship?**

    ❏ No gods
    ❏ Looks
    ❏ The gods of Mormonism
    ❏ Jesus
    ❏ The higher self—humans have everything inside them to live well
    ❏ The god of materialism
    ❏ Other: _____

5. **Erin lay on her bed turning the pages of a fashion magazine. She would be starting eighth grade in a few weeks, and it was so important to look good. She would definitely need some of the new shorter skirts and some boots.** *I need to look like I'm in eighth grade,* **she thought.** *I need to know what's "in" now and look more mature.*

    Do you think Erin is preoccupied with her looks? Do you think she will grow closer to or farther away from Jesus?

READ OUT LOUD

There is a cycle of behavior in the book of Judges: The people drift from faithfulness to God to faithlessness. They worship false gods, abandoning worship of the true God YHWH. So God allows them to become subject to the very things they are worshiping—and then they suffer. And when they cry out to God in repentance, God raises up a deliverer to rescue them. Barak and Deborah rose to the occasion and ruthlessly trusted in God. Gideon's faith response was a little different: He was initially reluctant and seemed less familiar with God than Barak or Deborah. God's assurance seemed insufficient, so Gideon demanded a sign. Then there was Jephthah. Not called by God, he was asked to serve by the elders (or leaders) in Israel. They were desperate and didn't wait for God. Jephthah wouldn't serve unless there was something in it for him. The view of God and faith was diminished as each generation went along. By the time of Jephthah, the people's view of God had badly deteriorated. While God used Jephthah to deliver the Israelites, we clearly see that Jephthah's faith was weak and his view of God distorted. Likewise we go from, "I'll go as long as the LORD goes before me" to "I need multiple assurances that I can do this" and then, "What's in it for me?" Read all about it in Judges 11:1-40.

ASK

Would you give money to a charity that would definitely save another kid's life if it meant you had to go without food for three days?

DISCUSS, BY THE NUMBERS

1. Jephthah was a self-absorbed man who had a distorted perspective of the God of the Bible. He would only serve God if there was something in it for him. Explore with your group members how we often approach our relationship with Christ in this way.
2. Use this activity to explore from whom and where your group members are learning about Jesus. Ask, "Do you live like what you've learned about Jesus is true?"

3. What or who you worship influences who you become. None of the answers makes you Christlike. It is only when we worship the Lord do we become more like Jesus. See the answers in bold after each statement to understand what we become:
   - When you worship money you become (rich, **greedy**, Christlike).
   - When you worship alcohol you become (**addicted**, popular, Christlike).
   - When you worship celebrities you become (important, **shallow**, Christlike).
   - When you worship looks you become (good looking, **self-absorbed**, Christlike).
   - When you worship friends you become (**insecure**, a loser, Christlike).
4. Use this activity as an opportunity to discuss the false gods in our culture, whether those gods are striving for wealth, the power of science and technology to save us, the mommy and daddy gods of a false religion like Mormonism, or the belief that our higher self is all we need.
5. Use this situation to help your group members talk about the things in their lives that distract them from their relationships with Christ.

THE CLOSE

Jephthah worshiped a god that was cold and distant, a god that needed to be cajoled into action and negotiated with to ensure favorable outcomes. He worshiped a god that would accept, even demand, a child sacrifice. And so Jephthah himself became such a man—a man who negotiated favorable outcomes for himself. He was a man who would even negotiate with the God of the universe. He didn't understand the God of love, of mercy, and of redemption. He only understood this petty, small god. Today we have the opportunity to choose to worship only the triune God of the Bible and become more like Jesus.

Is God Like a Genie in a Bottle?

God does not exist to bless what we do or give us what we desire

1. **In Israel during Micah's day the people did whatever they thought was right. What would happen at your school if nobody followed the rules? What would happen in your family? In your town?**

   In those days Israel had no king; everyone did as they saw fit. (Judges 17:6)

2. **Jesus is like a genie in a bottle. Rub the bottle and get your three wishes.**

   ❏ I totally agree.
   ❏ I mostly agree.
   ❏ I mostly disagree.
   ❏ I totally disagree.

3. **I am like Micah's mom because I get other people to worship idols.**

   ❏ That's me   ❏ That's not me

4. **What's your opinion?**

   ❏ Jesus always does what I want him to do.
   ❏ Jesus mostly does what I want him to do.
   ❏ Jesus sometimes does what I want him to do.
   ❏ Jesus never does what I want him to do.
   ❏ Jesus' job isn't doing what I want him to do.

5. **What do you think? Y (yes) or N (no)**

   ___ God is far away from me.
   ___ I need to worship God because God is worthy to be worshiped.
   ___ God lives in our church's sanctuary.
   ___ God's job is to serve me.
   ___ God was surprised by the creation of the universe through random chance and time.
   ___ If I follow all the rules, then God will give me what I want.
   ___ God is three-in-one.
   ___ God is a very big and powerful God who does what he pleases.
   ___ God knows what is best for me even more than I do.
   ___ There is a God—and I'm not him.

6. **Chad listened to the pastor really hard when he was talking about praying. He liked what he heard. All he had to do was pray and God would answer his prayers. Cool. As soon as Chad got home he asked God about that video game he'd been wanting.**

   What's wrong with Chad's view of God?

READ OUT LOUD

Micah, who stole from his own mother, gave the stolen silver back. His mother, happy to have her silver back, asked God to bless Micah . . . but then cast the silver to an idol. She had a distorted view of the God of the Bible. This perverted view of God was passed along to her son, Micah, and to her grandson. Micah created a shrine to a false god then thought the Lord would bless what he did and give him what he wanted. Micah was not an atheist. He did believe in God. But Micah had a distorted view of God, just like his mother. Read the details in Judges 17:1-13.

ASK

If a genie popped out of a bottle and gave you three wishes, for what would you wish?

DISCUSS, BY THE NUMBERS

1. Read Judges 17:6 out loud. Micah did what he wanted because God was no longer the ruler or king of Israel. Everyone did what they thought was right in their own eyes. God's way of doing things was no longer their absolute moral standard. Discuss with your group members what would happen if everyone in their school, families, and your town acted like Micah.

> *In those days Israel had no king; everyone did as they saw fit. (Judges 17:6)*

2. Too often, we see Jesus as our genie in a bottle. Even those not committed to Christ as Savior and Lord take this perspective. Talk together about how this viewpoint is counter to Scripture and harmful to our relationships with Christ. God wants what's best for us—and that is only achieved when we're obedient to Jesus. As Christ-followers we have the privilege of serving Jesus rather than our own self-centered interests.

3. We are either influencing our friends and family to follow Christ or influencing them to follow something else. Most of your group members haven't thought about this concept before. Make a list together of what or who we influence others to follow if not Christ—money, popularity, pop stars, fashion, and more.

4. Challenge your group to think about what they do to attempt to get Jesus to do what they want. How often do they promise God that they will go to church if God gives them good grades? How often do they try to do good deeds so that God will answer prayers? How often do they read their Bibles so that God will do what they want? Talk together about the frustrations you and your group members have felt when God doesn't answer your prayers the way you wanted God to answer them. In today's story, Micah and his mother thought that God could be manipulated. Let's get a proper perspective of God—who does *not* exist to serve us. Rather we have been created to have a relationship with and serve God.

5. In today's story, we see that Micah had a distorted view of God. God's name was thrown around recklessly, but God didn't seem to make an appearance to Micah. See the commentary in bold to get a bigger and better picture of God than Micah's picture:

- God is far away from me. **Actually, Jesus is present in our lives all the time through the Holy Spirit who lives in all Christ-followers.**
- I need to worship God because God is worthy to be worshiped. **God created all things, including us. That makes God worthy of our worship.**
- God lives in our church's sanctuary. **This is a misnomer. The church building where we worship should not be called the sanctuary. God lives in our hearts.**
- God's job is to serve me. **No. My job is to serve God.**
- God was surprised by the creation of the universe through random chance and time. **No. Nothing surprises the God who created the universe.**
- If I follow all the rules, then God will give me what I want. **God gives us what we *need*. We shouldn't be "good" by following all the rules in the hopes of manipulating God.**
- God is three-in-one. **Yes. God exists as three persons in one.**
- God is a very big and powerful God who does what he pleases. **Yes. And what God pleases is always holy and right.**
- God knows what is best for me even more than I do. **Yes. That's why we can put our complete trust in God.**
- There is a God—and I'm not him. **Yes. Although we often play God when we take things into our own hands.**

6. This true-to-life situation gives you one more chance to drive home the big idea that God does not exist to bless what we do or give us what we desire.

THE CLOSE

We read the story of Micah, and we might thank God that we are not like him. But let's not be too hasty. How often do we believe that God exists to meet our needs and give us what we want when we want it? Let's remember that God is not some genie in a bottle. God is the creator of all things. God has a claim on our lives. God wants to have a personal relationship with us. It's much more than what God might give to us.

1. Do you think the following statements are true (T) or false (F)?

___ Samson should never have desired what he wasn't supposed to have.
___ God didn't want any Israelite marrying a Philistine because God is against having fun.
___ God wanted the Philistines to go to hell.
___ God knew what was best for Samson.
___ Samson teaches us that you can have what is not good for you.

Getting Caught Up in the Culture

What does it mean to be "set apart for God"?

2. **What do you think?**

I would never act like Samson.	❏ YES	❏ NO	❏ MAYBE
I wish I was as strong as Samson.	❏ YES	❏ NO	❏ MAYBE
I know people like Samson.	❏ YES	❏ NO	❏ MAYBE

3. **People who are focused on what the world has to offer—**

❏ are missing out.　　　❏ really know how to live.

4. **Christian teenagers should date—**

❏ as many people as possible.
❏ only when they graduate from high school.
❏ nice people.
❏ people with a lot of money.

❏ only followers of Jesus.
❏ who they can convince to come to their church.
❏ great kissers.

5. **Samson was to be set apart from birth, to belong to God (Judges 13:3-16). For me, "set apart" for God means (M for more or L for less)—**

Watch _____ TV than I do now.
Play _____ games than I do now.
Send and receive _____ texts than I do now.
Spend _____ time surfing the Web than I do now.
Read the Bible _____ than I do now.
Spend _____ time with social media than I do now.

Read _____ teen magazines than I do now.
Pray _____ than I do now.
Go to _____ movies than I do now.
Spend _____ time with the people in my congregation than I do now.

6. "Everybody lies to their parents," said Scott. "We're kids; it's what we do."
   Tim shook his head.
   "Come on Tim," said Scott, sounding more and more frustrated. "You know you want to go."
   Of course Tim wanted to go with his friends; it was just something his parents wouldn't approve of. Even though Scott would be angry, Tim wouldn't lie to his parents.

   Do you think Scott is making the right decision? What do you think Scott should tell Tim? Do you have friends like Scott? Like Tim?

READ OUT LOUD

The story of Samson is a tragic warning for us. His parents were told that their son belonged to God—that the Lord would use him to free Israel from the grip of their enemy, the Philistines. God's Holy Spirit was with Samson, but unfortunately Samson chose to act on his own rather than surrender his life to God. Read the story from Judges to see how Samson refused to be set apart for God and instead indulged himself in the ways of the world.

ASK

How often do you get what you want?

DISCUSS, BY THE NUMBERS

1. See commentary in bold after each statement:
   - Samson should never have desired what he wasn't supposed to have. Samson knew that God wanted him to serve Israel. **Samson had an important job, but his desires got in the way of doing God's will and ultimately harmed him.**
   - God didn't want any Israelite marrying a Philistine because God is against having fun. **God wanted the Israelites to marry other God-followers, not to limit their fun but to protect their marriages and their children.**
   - God wanted the Philistines to go to hell. **No, the Philistines were sending themselves to hell by their stubborn refusal to follow the one true God, the God of the Bible.**
   - God knew what was best for Samson. **Of course God knew what was best. Yet, Samson stubbornly followed his own appetites and ambitions rather than God's will.**
   - Samson teaches us that you can have what is not good for you. **Quite the opposite is true. Samson's life shows us that the good life is a life lived for God and others rather than self.**
2. Discuss what moves us from *acting like Samson* to *not acting like Samson*. Ask, "What do we need to do to *never act like Samson*?" "Why can we be jealous of people like Samson who seem to always get whatever they want, even when it hurts others?" Point out that Samson may have been physically strong, but he was morally, emotionally, and spiritually weak. You can predict what will happen to people who are like Samson—they ultimately end up shallow and lonely.
3. The perception held by many Christians is that they are missing out because they are not "worldly." Use this activity to discuss what people who are "worldly" miss out on by not embracing Jesus. Explore how Christians are the ones who really know how to live. Also talk about how we are to "be in the world but not of the world." Ask, "How much are we to participate in worldly things?" This is an age-old question that you will not answer definitively with your group. However, wrestling with the question will help your group members as they struggle in the future with how to live for Christ.
4. The discussion can easily move away from today's topic of being set apart for God. Do let your group tell their stories and share their opinions. However, try to keep boundaries around the discussion to stay focused on God's will for our lives rather than who is a "hottie." The Old Testament forbade the people of God to marry Philistines (i.e., in a broader sense, those who aren't God-followers) for a reason. God knew then and knows now that marrying someone outside of the faith usually leads the Christian away from faith rather than the outsider coming to the faith. Idolatry, a primary focus on someone or something other than God, leads us away from Jesus Christ. This can happen in our dating lives, too.
5. Use this activity to look practically at what it means for Christians today to be "set apart."
6. Use this true-to-life situation to identify real-life situations your group members face.

THE CLOSE

We don't often think of ourselves as set apart for God's purposes. When we do think of a purposeful life lived for Christ, we struggle with how much we should engage our culture or run from it. Yet, here we are, stuck in a culture that doesn't honor God or embrace Jesus as Lord. How do we live in the world without the world living in us?

The Samson & Delilah Disaster

Getting to know someone from the inside out

1. "He is so cute," said Maria. She and her friend Elizabeth were looking at pictures of a popular singer on a well-known celebrity Web site. "I bet he's an amazing person."

   "I know," said Elizabeth. "You can just tell from looking at him that he's a really nice guy. Articles about him make him sound so friendly. I wish I had a boyfriend like him."

   "I wonder if what they say about him is true," said Maria.

   What's wrong with the way Maria and Elizabeth are thinking about boyfriend relationships?

2. Samson kept practicing the same sins over and over again—apparently not learning anything that would change his sinful behavior. What have you learned from your past sins? You can check more than one box.

   ❏ I don't seem to have learned anything because I keep doing them over and over.
   ❏ Don't get caught again.
   ❏ Make better friendship choices.
   ❏ My sins were stupid decisions.
   ❏ What I got from my sins wasn't worth committing them.

   ❏ Don't repeat the same sins over and over.
   ❏ Treat people with more respect.
   ❏ I have trouble admitting that my sins are sins because everyone else is doing them, too.
   ❏ I need God's help to change my sinful behavior.
   ❏ Temptation is really strong.

3. Delilah was in a relationship with Samson for what she could get out of it. The same could be said for Samson. How do you treat your friends?

   ❏ I gossip about them.
   ❏ I tell them only what they want to hear.
   ❏ I get what I can from them and move on.
   ❏ I treat them like I want to be treated.

   ❏ I dump them if they don't do everything I want.
   ❏ I'm honest with them.
   ❏ I talk with them about my faith.

4. Samson trusted in his own strength rather than relying on the Lord. What things do you try to control because you believe you can handle them on your own?

   ❏ Athletics
   ❏ Getting along with people at school or after school
   ❏ TV viewing

   ❏ Internet use
   ❏ Relationship with parents
   ❏ Getting along with friends
   ❏ School work

5. Cory stopped at the classroom door. Every eye in her science class was focused on her. Okay, so she'd lost a little weight over the summer between 7th and 8th grade; actually *a lot* of weight. Joining the summer swim team and eating less really made a difference. Now all the guys were staring at her in the halls and wanting to sit by her. It was weird. She was still the same person she was last year when hardly anyone talked to her.

   What was the sin of Cory's classmates? Do you think her "friends" will learn from their sin?

READ OUT LOUD

Samson was a judge in Israel for 20 years. He conquered Israel's enemy, the Philistines, again and again. Yet he was never able to conquer his selfish desires. When he saw something he wanted, he took it. Samson allowed his lust for a woman who didn't follow God to distract him from the purpose of his life. Read all about it in Judges 16:4-22.

ASK

What distracts you the most from getting your homework done on time?

DISCUSS, BY THE NUMBERS

1. Use this true-to-life situation to discuss the importance of getting to know someone from the inside out. Maria and Elizabeth really didn't know the celebrity beyond a few outward qualities. Yet they assumed he must be nice. Our culture emphasizes outward looks rather than inward beauty. Many in our culture jump to the physical in relationships before getting to know each other spiritually, emotionally, and intellectually.

2. Lead a faith conversation on how we can choose or not choose to learn from our own sins as well as the sins of others. There is an emphasis in our culture today to learn how not to get caught rather than how we can change our behavior. Perhaps we need to make better friendship choices or learn how to treat people with more respect. Maybe we need to see how stupid our decisions were when we look back on them—that our sins weren't worth it. We might also learn to surrender our temptations and sins to God, asking Christ to change our sinful behavior.

3. For each of the statements ask, "How does this honor God in your relationship?" Samson didn't seem to care much about God's opinion in his relationships. Ask, "How much does God's opinion mean to you when you consider your friendship relationships?"

4. This can be a difficult concept for young people to comprehend. They think they don't have to rely on the Lord because it seems like they can handle most things themselves. They haven't lived long enough to realize that human control is an illusion. It is God who gave us our abilities, talents, smarts, or looks. It is God who can use these to work in us and through us for his purposes. When we surrender these to Jesus, then Jesus can use them for his glory. When we use them for our selfish goals, then it's all about us and our desires. Samson trusted in his own strength and abilities to get what he wanted. It ended in disaster. Imagine what might have happened if Samson would have used his strength and abilities to glorify God. Think how many people could have been helped—how the world could have been a better place with Samson submitting himself to God.

5. Use this true-to-life situation to talk about real situations in which we judge others. Ask, "What can we learn from these sins?"

THE CLOSE

Samson (and the Philistines) kept repeating sins, apparently not willing to learn from them. When we don't reflect on our sinful actions, as well as God's opinion of them, we fall into a trap of repeating our sins with their growing negative consequences. Unlike Samson, we can choose to learn from our sinful behaviors. We can choose to change as we surrender those sins to God.

Dagon Captures Samson

Giving credit to Jesus

1. The Philistines gave credit to Dagon, their god, for helping them capture Samson. Today, to whom or what do most people in the U.S. give credit for our high standard of living?

   ❏ Their abilities, strength, brains, money, or looks
   ❏ Jesus Christ
   ❏ Science and technology
   ❏ The universe
   ❏ Hard work

2. Do you think the following statements are T (true) or F (false)?

   ___ I like owning the latest and best cell phone.
   ___ I best communicate with my friends through technology.
   ___ I've sacrificed my (or my parents') money to own the latest technology.
   ___ I tell all my friends when I get new technology.
   ___ My bedroom is filled with technology.

3. Jesus taught that we ought to love our enemies. The Philistines practiced the opposite of Jesus' command. They hated and made fun of Samson. I love my enemies—

   ❏ all the time.   ❏ hardly ever.
   ❏ most of the time.   ❏ never.
   ❏ sometimes.

4. Samson was blind, beat up, and chained when he turned to God for help. Does it take bad things happening to you before you pray, read your Bible, and turn to Christ for guidance?

   ❏ Never   ❏ Often
   ❏ Sometimes   ❏ Always

5. Ethan was watching a sports awards show. Each athlete who won an award got on stage and gave a little speech. They all thanked their families and coaches and their teammates. But one guy was different. He got up and said that he would like to "thank Jesus Christ and give him all the glory." That seemed different. It probably took a lot of guts for the guy to get in front of all those other athletes and thank Jesus. Ethan was intrigued.

   Why would an athlete give a thank you to Jesus Christ?

READ OUT LOUD

Delilah, Samson's girlfriend, had lured him into her trap. She learned the secret of his strength—his long hair—and gave him a haircut. With his strength sapped, Samson was easily overtaken by his Philistine enemies who blinded him and threw him into prison. Read the rest of the story found in Judges 16:23-31.

ASK

What is one secret you were unable to keep?

DISCUSS, BY THE NUMBERS

1. See commentary in bold after each statement:
   - Their abilities, strength, brains, money, or looks. **Instead of being humbled by what God has given us and done for us, we too often take credit for something that God blessed us with.**
   - Jesus Christ. **Only by honoring Jesus, the maker of our universe and the giver of all good things, do we give credit where credit is due.**
   - Science and technology. **We certainly spend a great deal of time and money on our phones, tablets, TVs, and computers. It's easy to worship at the feet of technology rather than seeing Jesus as the source of life and truth.**
   - The universe. **This is a new-age concept that says we're mystically connected to the universe (which also lives inside of us). This belief distracts people from Jesus Christ as the source of life and gives a false impression of self-importance.**
   - Hard work. **While hard work is important, false pride can show up—and that's not good, as it honors self and humankind's achievements apart from God.**

2. The Philistines threw a big party to celebrate their god Dagon's victory over Samson. Each of the statements is an example of how we can get caught up in the worship of the god of technology. Ask, "How can we use today's technology without worshiping it?"

3. Read Matthew 5:43-44 out loud. Talk about what makes it so difficult to love our enemies even though Christ taught us to do so. Ask, "What can you practice doing that would help you love your enemies—pray for them, stop gossiping about them, forgive them, make peace with them, help them when they need help?"

> *"You have heard that it was said, 'Love your neighbor and hate your enemy.' But I tell you, love your enemies and pray for those who persecute you." (Matthew 5:43-44)*

4. Give an example of what needs to happen in your life to get you to pray, read your Bible, or turn to Christ more for guidance. It took a disaster to get Samson to turn to God. After talking about how often it takes bad things happening before we pray, read our Bibles, or turn to Christ for guidance, discuss how we can make these normal routines in our lives.

5. Use this true-to-life situation to talk about giving credit to Jesus for the abilities, brains, money, talent, and discipline to do what we need to do in order to be successful *for Christ* rather than for ourselves.

THE CLOSE

The Philistines gave credit to a false god for their successful capture of Samson. And Samson gave credit to himself for much of his life. In the end Samson turned back to God but unfortunately wasted much of his life in selfish pursuits. We can spend our lives preoccupied with ourselves, our technology, and our shallow culture of worldliness—or we can give credit to Jesus Christ for working in us and through us to bring about God's kingdom. We can pursue a life of selfish ambition or realize our brokenness and rely on Christ for our successes.

Naomi & Ruth Lose Loved Ones

Bad things happen even to followers of Christ

1. Do you agree (A) or disagree (D) with the following statements?

___ Life was unfair for Naomi and Ruth.
___ Bad things happen to good people.
___ God set the world in motion but is unable to stop evil from happening.
___ Naomi and Ruth deserved what they got.
___ Sin caused the suffering experienced by Naomi and Ruth.
___ Life is filled with tragedy . . . then you die.

2. Eddie and his grandfather were buddies. His grandfather took Eddie fishing, taught him how to play the guitar, and played chess with him. They really enjoyed being together. But lately his grandfather started to act strangely. He called Eddie by his father's name. Last weekend he even forgot that he could play chess! Eddie's mom told him that his grandfather had a disease called *Alzheimer's.*

Why do you think something like this could happen to a good guy like Eddie's grandfather?

3. Ruth's friends barely recognized her when she returned to Israel (see Ruth 1:19). She was sad, broke, and had no place to live. Who do you think would notice you if you were hurting?

❏ Parent
❏ Teacher
❏ Brother or sister
❏ Best friend

❏ Sunday school teacher
❏ Coach
❏ Acquaintance

4. Why do you suppose bad things happen to good people like Naomi and Ruth? (You can choose more than one answer.)

❏ They are secretly Satan worshipers.
❏ Nobody knows for sure.
❏ Because we live in a world filled with sin—and often that sin spills over to hurt us.
❏ God wants to teach these people something.
❏ It's God's punishment for their sins.
❏ Because life is not always fair.
❏ Bad things happen to followers of Christ and those who don't follow Christ.

5. If something really bad happened to me like what happened to Naomi and Ruth, I think I would—

❏ run from God.
❏ get closer to God.
❏ stop believing in God altogether.

READ OUT LOUD

Bad things happen to everyone—atheists, agnostics, Muslims, Jews, Christians. They happened to Naomi, a Jewish woman whose family was forced out of Israel by a severe famine. Her husband died. Then her two sons died. As a woman in a patriarchal society she had no one to care for her, to protect her. She was doomed to a life of poverty. Read the story found in Ruth 1:1-22.

ASK

What is the worst thing that has happened to you during school hours?

DISCUSS, BY THE NUMBERS

1. See commentary in bold after each statement:
   - Life was unfair for Naomi and Ruth. **It certainly seemed unfair for Naomi and Ruth. The fact is that life is often difficult. We like to fool ourselves (especially if we live in wealthy nations) into thinking that life should always be fun.**
   - Bad things happen to good people. **Bad things happen to everyone—whether you or I or they follow Christ or not. It is an unavoidable part of being human.**
   - God set the world in motion but is unable to stop evil from happening. **God can do whatever God wants. God is intimately involved in the world, including in each of our lives. Evil is caused by sin. There are billions of people in the world, which makes sin pervasive.**
   - Naomi and Ruth deserved what they got. **If we all got what we deserved, we would be in hell. No, God was gracious to Naomi and Ruth just as God is gracious to followers of Christ. God's common grace benefits all of humankind.**
   - Sin caused the suffering experienced by Naomi and Ruth. **We can look for sinfulness in the lives of Naomi and Ruth, but this doesn't seem to be what the book of Ruth is communicating to us.**
   - Life is filled with tragedy . . . then you die. **Life is filled with suffering and tragedies and then you grow—if you choose (see James 1:2-4).**

2. Use this true-to-life situation to discuss the reality of suffering in our world. Life is difficult, but as followers of Christ, we have the Holy Spirit (also called the Comforter) with us to walk through the suffering. We won't always avoid suffering. Neither will those who don't follow Christ. We will, however, have each other in the church and the Holy Spirit with us.

3. Naomi went from a member of a well-to-do and respected family to a single woman living in poverty. Barely recognizable by her former friends, she was destitute. Find out why the people your group members chose would notice them hurting. Ask, "What do you do when you notice others hurting?"

4. Why do you think bad things happen to good people like Naomi and Ruth? (You can choose more than one answer.) See commentary in bold after each statement:
   - They are secretly Satan worshipers. **Usually not the case.**
   - Nobody knows for sure. **This response reminds us of the book of Job where God never revealed to Job (but did to us) the reason for his suffering.**
   - Because we live in a world filled with sin—and often that sin spills over to hurt us. **There is no escaping the reality of our fallen nature. All of humanity is broken by sin. This sinfulness causes great suffering even for those who don't deserve the suffering (e.g., infants).**
   - God wants to teach these people something. **James 1:2-4 and other biblical references point out that God uses suffering for character development—to mature us to be more like Jesus.**
   - It's God's punishment for their sins. **Christians may be disciplined for their sins, but the punishment has been paid for by Jesus.**
   - Because life is not always fair. **Life is unfair, and some people suffer more than others through no fault of their own.**
   - Bad things happen to followers of Christ and those who don't follow Christ. **Bad things happen to everyone. Jesus said that it rains on the just and the unjust (see Matthew 5:45).**

5. Discuss why some people would run from God while others would get closer to God and still others would stop believing in God altogether.

THE CLOSE

Naomi faced more trouble than she seemed to deserve. Yet she kept her belief in God, and her faith remained intact. She knew that she served a good God who could have prevented the bad from happening. The God she served was a God who did all things for a reason. While she didn't see the big picture of why this was happening to her, she trusted that God knew. She understood that God loved her and in fact wanted the best for her. We know the ending of the story that Naomi never saw. God used her family, through Ruth, to bring us Jesus Christ, her Savior, our Savior, the Savior of the world.

1. **Ruth showed Naomi a dependable, sacrificial love—the kind of love God shows to us. When have you shown this compassionate kind of love to others?**

   - ❏ I never do.
   - ❏ I don't understand this kind of love.
   - ❏ I don't know how to show this kind of love.
   - ❏ This is something you do only when you are older.
   - ❏ I show this kind of love all the time.
   - ❏ Sometimes I show this kind of love.

2. **God provided Old Testament laws to protect and care for the poor—people like Ruth and Naomi. What do you think?**

   God still works on behalf of the poor.　❏ I agree.　❏ I disagree.　❏ I have no idea.

3. **It was no coincidence that Ruth ended up in Boaz's field. God, working behind the scenes, made it happen. What do you think?** *What look like coincidences in my life are often God working behind the scenes.*

   - ❏ Always
   - ❏ Most of the time
   - ❏ Sometimes
   - ❏ Hardly ever
   - ❏ Never

4. **What do you think?**

I often act like Boaz who always tried to do what was right.	❏ YES	❏ NO	❏ MAYBE
I have friends like Boaz.	❏ YES	❏ NO	❏ MAYBE
There are people in my congregation like Boaz.	❏ YES	❏ NO	❏ MAYBE

5. **By the time the "new kid" sat down on the bus next to Andrew that afternoon, Andrew pretty much knew all about him. Word travels fast in their small school. Andrew knew the kid was from out of town and that he was living with his mom since his parents got divorced.**
   He looks kind of lonely, **thought Andrew. Oh no! This was one of those situations that the pastor had been talking about, the one where God gives you a chance to do something.** *Okay*, **he concluded,** *maybe I'll talk to him someday.*
   The bus stopped and Andrew got up—and so did the new kid.
   He lives on my street! Okay God, I get it, this is the day.
   "Hey," said Andrew, as they got off the bus. "My name is Andrew. What's yours?"

   When was the last time you experienced a situation in which you later realized God had set up for you to do something spectacular for him? How did you (or didn't you) take advantage of the situation?

READ OUT LOUD

We use words like *coincidence* or *chance* as if God has nothing to do with the situations—as if things just happen randomly or by accident. Yet in today's account, what looks like a random meeting is really God working in the background. God is God no matter how bad things look to us, and God is alive and well working on our behalf to do his will. Read what happened in Ruth 2:1-23.

ASK

Do you think people your age like to be in front of others or be in the background?

DISCUSS, BY THE NUMBERS

1. God showed us *hesed* (his lovingkindness to us, his creatures) by sending Jesus to die for our sins. Talk with your group about a time other than Jesus' death and resurrection when you experienced God's *hesed*. God wants us to share his sacrificial lovingkindness with others. Ask for stories of how your group members have shared and received *hesed* from others.

2. Yes, God still works on behalf of the poor. During the time of Ruth, God required farmers to allow the poor to take the extra grain left in a field after the reapers had finished their harvesting—it's called "gleaning" and is still practiced today. God cared about the poor in the Old Testament, and he cares about the poor today. There are hundreds of verses in the Bible that address God's concern for the poor, as well as God's desire for us to be his hands and feet in helping the poor. But God is not working only on behalf of the poor; God is working on behalf of all his children to make us more like Jesus as he carries out his will in our lives.

3. It was no coincidence that Ruth ended up in Boaz's field. Ruth had no idea that she would end up there, but the author of this book of the Bible wants us to know that God led her to that field. People back then or even today could call it *coincidence*, but we see from the outcome of the story of Ruth that God had a plan. God often shows up in our lives working behind the scenes in ways that we won't understand until later. We do have the completed Bible, so we can see God intimately involved with his people. More often than not, it's only when we look back that we see God's hand moving in our lives. God is using all situations in our lives for our good and the good of God's kingdom (see Romans 8:28). Talk about examples of how, when you look back, you see God was working behind the scenes in your life.

4. For both young people and adults, we can act totally like Boaz one day and then turn into the opposite the next day. That's why God is working in the lives of Christians for our good (*sanctification*). Discuss who your group members identified as their role models (both peers and adults) who can help them become more like Boaz, a man of integrity.

5. Use this true-to-life situation to talk practically about how God is working behind the scenes in the lives of your group members.

THE CLOSE

When we first meet Ruth in the Bible, we see a disaster. Nothing is going right. God seems to have abandoned her and her mother-in-law Naomi. It looks like there is no end in sight to her misery. God, however, was working in the background to influence Ruth and those around her for Ruth's benefit. God is doing the same in our lives. We need to put our trust in God, who has our best interests at heart. Even the tough times can be used by God for our benefit. So, like Ruth, we can have faith in Christ to work his will in our lives.

1. **God was involved in the details of Ruth and Boaz's future before they ever met each other.**

   ❑ I want Jesus involved in my future.
   ❑ I'm not sure if I want Jesus involved in my future.
   ❑ I don't want Jesus messing with my future.

9. Ruth 4:13-22

Boaz Marries Ruth

God has a plan for you—a plan you may not yet perceive

2. **God was working out his plan in the life of Ruth and Boaz—a big plan that led to the birth of Christ. Do you think the following statements are T (true) of F (false)?**

   ___ God doesn't have a plan for my life because I'm too young.
   ___ I don't think about God's plan for my life.
   ___ God doesn't work out life plans today like he did in the days of Ruth and Boaz.
   ___ God has a plan for my life, but I can't see it yet.
   ___ I trust that God has a plan for my life that is best for me.

3. **Both Ruth and Boaz were God-followers who willingly did what was right in God's eyes rather than whatever they thought was right. I'm like Ruth and Boaz—**

   ❑ all the time.   ❑ hardly ever.
   ❑ most of the time.   ❑ never.
   ❑ sometimes.

4. **Who first told you about Jesus?**

   ❑ Parent   ❑ Sunday school teacher
   ❑ Grandparent   ❑ Youth worker
   ❑ Other family member   ❑ Teacher
   ❑ Pastor   ❑ Coach
   ❑ Friend   ❑ Other: _____
   ❑ Neighbor

5. **Bonnie had a plan. She and her new friend Casey were going to have a great summer. They were going to go to the mall, watch movies, and swim. It was going to be awesome. Casey even said she would come to church with Bonnie and her family. It was going to be so cool! Then Casey got sick, really sick. She was in the hospital for two weeks and was going to have to spend most of the summer recovering. Most of the summer! So much for their plans.** *Now what am I going to do?* **thought Bonnie.** *This was going to be such a great summer. Not now.*

   How might God be working on Bonnie's behalf even though she doesn't see it?

READ OUT LOUD

The famine was over, so Naomi returned with Ruth to Israel after having lost everything. Naomi blamed God for her and Ruth's predicament, not knowing that God had a plan that she couldn't yet see. Empty-handed and hungry Ruth picked the leftover grain from the field of Boaz to provide enough food for her and Naomi. Without knowing that God was working behind the scenes on her behalf, Ruth got to know Boaz, who eventually married her. Read the story found in Ruth 4:13-22.

ASK

Do your parents plan vacations in detail or just go someplace with no idea where your family will stay or what you'll do?

DISCUSS, BY THE NUMBERS

1. Ruth had no idea what God had planned for her when she left her country with her mother-in-law Ruth and journeyed to Israel. She left her gods for the God of the Bible. She left her family and friends for the unknown. She couldn't see what her future held. She trusted in God, willing to believe that he had a plan for her life that she couldn't yet see. Your group members can't see the future that God has planned for them, either, but they can choose to trust in Jesus now. They can walk with Jesus as he leads them into the future, believing that he will be with them.

2. Genealogies are in the Bible to connect the generations in a way that gives us a message. The genealogy at the end of today's story connects Ruth and Boaz to King David which connects them to Jesus Christ. God's plan for Ruth and Boaz included the salvation of Israel. Through them God worked out an elaborate plan to save not only Israel but also the world—because of Christ's death and resurrection. See commentary in bold after each statement:

   • God doesn't have a plan for my life because I'm too young. **If you have given your life to Christ, then God is working out a plan for your life even though you can't yet see it or believe you are too young for God to have a plan for you.**

   • I don't think about God's plan for my life. **If you are growing in your relationship with Christ, you will be thinking of God's plan for your future and how you need to prepare for that plan.**

   • God doesn't work out life plans today like he did in the days of Ruth and Boaz. **God works today like he did in Old Testament times. God is causing some things to happen and allowing others to happen and weaving them all together for your good to bring his kingdom to earth.**

   • God has a plan for my life, but I can't see it yet. **While we can't always tell or understand what God is doing, don't be fooled into believing God has abandoned you. God hasn't—just as he didn't abandon Naomi or Ruth, even though it appeared differently.**

   • I trust that God has a plan for my life that is best for me. **Continue to put your faith in Christ and watch God do great things through you.**

3. Ruth and Boaz were people of substance who challenge us to be Christ-followers with character who do what God wants. Discuss why willingly doing what is right in God's eyes rather than whatever we think is right makes us people of substance, too.

4. Ask, "Has the Christian faith been passed on to you—have you put your faith in Christ?"

5. Use this true-to-life situation to talk about real issues your group members face.

THE CLOSE

The writer of the book of Ruth wanted us to clearly see God operating behind the scenes to work out his plan for the salvation of the world through Ruth and Boaz. Through them Christ was eventually born. It first appears that God didn't seem to be looking out for Naomi and Ruth, but by chapter four we find God's complex plan working out. God is doing no less in our lives. We must put our faith in Christ, knowing that God is causing some events to happen while allowing others—and in the end weaves a plan for our lives that gives glory to God.

A "Yes" Answer

God answers our prayers with "yes," "no," or "wait"

1. What do you think? YES or NO . . .

God only listens to the prayers of good people.
❏ YES   ❏ NO

God usually says "NO" to my prayer requests.
❏ YES   ❏ NO

God listens to the prayers of adults more than kids.
❏ YES   ❏ NO

There is no reason to pray because God already knows what I need.
❏ YES   ❏ NO

God does what God wants whether I pray or don't pray.
❏ YES   ❏ NO

2. I pray only when I'm in trouble.

❏ That's always me.   ❏ That's sometimes me.
❏ That's usually me.   ❏ That's not me at all.

3. Hannah prayed for a long time. How long do you usually pray? (Check one.)

❏ Less than a minute   ❏ Longer than 15 minutes
❏ Less than five minutes   ❏ An hour or more at a time
❏ Five to 15 minutes

4. *God must not want our family to be happy,* thought Mary before she prayed. Mary prayed every night before she went to sleep that her parents would stop fighting. Mary figured that if they just stopped fighting then maybe they would remember that they loved each other and things wouldn't always be so tense around their home. But Mary had been praying for a while, and they were still fighting. *What's the use?* she thought, climbing in bed and turning out the light. *Tonight I will just go straight to sleep.*

Why do you think Mary is ready to give up on prayer?
Why do you think God might not make Mary's parents quit fighting even though she has earnestly prayed for this to happen?
For what do you think Mary should pray?

5. Hannah showed her gratitude for God's answered prayer by naming her son Samuel, which means "God heard." When (and for what) do you thank God? Check all that apply.

❏ I thank God when I get a YES answer to prayer.
❏ I thank God when I get a NO answer to prayer.
❏ I thank God when I get a WAIT answer to prayer.
❏ I forget to thank God.
❏ I don't pray.

READ OUT LOUD

Polygamy was accepted in some Old Testament times—a man could have more than one wife. However, as we read the Old Testament, we see that in families in which husbands had more than one wife were filled with conflict. Today's story is no different. A man named Elkanah—a God-follower—had two wives, Peninnah and Hannah. Let the rivalry begin! Hannah was her husband's favorite. She prayed for a child, and God answered with a "yes." Read the story found in 1 Samuel 1:1-20.

ASK

Do your parents say "yes" to you more than they say "no"?

DISCUSS, BY THE NUMBERS

1. See commentary in bold after each statement:
   - God only listens to the prayers of good people. **If this were true, nobody's prayers would be heard. Fortunately, there is grace.**
   - God usually says "NO" to my prayer requests. **Often young people believe this is true. Introduce the notion here that God will always answer our prayers with a "yes" or a "no" or a "wait."**
   - God listens to the prayers of adults more than kids. **No. God listens to the prayers of the youth in your congregation as well as to the adults' prayers.**
   - There is no reason to pray because God already knows what I need. **God already knows what we need, true—but God wants us to pray because God wants a friendship with us! God just wants to hear our voices, our hearts. Jesus tells you in Matthew 6:9 that "your Father knows what you need before you ask him. This, then, is how you should pray," Jesus said before he uttered what we call the Lord's Prayer.**
   - God does what God wants whether I pray or don't pray. **Many passages of Scripture speak of God changing his mind. This means that, as part of our friendship with God, we are to pray because our prayers are important to God.**

2. **"The only time I pray is when I'm in trouble"** is a common condition of the prayer lives of both young people and adults. Ask, "How can we discipline ourselves to pray in all of life's circumstances?" Talk about how you would answer this question.

3. Explore the amount of time your group members spend in prayer. Point out that how long we pray isn't as important as the fact that we are praying. Jesus wants a relationship with us. Prayer is vital to that relationship growing.

4. See commentary in bold after each question:
   - Why do you think Mary is ready to give up on prayer? **Mary isn't seeing instant results. In our society we expect instant everything. God often answers our prayers with a "wait."**
   - Why do you think God might not make Mary's parents quit fighting even though she has earnestly prayed for this to happen? **God has given each of us a free will. Mary's parents can choose to change or keep fighting. This choice is not up to God.**
   - For what do you think Mary should pray? **Mary could pray that God would help her better understand her parents' situation. She could pray that God would place others in her parents' lives that could help them. She could pray that God would give her strength to endure this difficult situation. (And of course she should continue to pray that God will heal her parents and help them hear God's voice.)**

5. Discuss with your group why we are so prone to thank God for "yes" answers but not so much for "no" or "wait" answers to our prayers.

THE CLOSE

The God of the universe loves to hear your prayers. Because God wants the best for you, God's answers are not always "yes." Sometimes what is best for you is a "no" answer. Think back to past prayers. What would your life be like if every one of your prayers was answered in the affirmative? See? If we don't always make the correct decisions, why would God grant our every request? God knows what is best for you.

Dedicated Dude

Who in your life is dedicated to your spiritual growth?

1. Many people during the time of this Old Testament account worshiped the sun, the moon, the stars, and the angels who lived in heaven. Elkanah, the father of Samuel, worshiped the God of the Bible, the God who created all things. Who do you know who always puts the God of the Bible first in their lives?

   ❏ One or both of my parents
   ❏ My grandparents
   ❏ My pastor
   ❏ My coach
   ❏ A friend
   ❏ A teacher
   ❏ Someone in my church

2. Samuel had a mother who was committed to praying for him. Who do you want praying for you?

   ❏ The prayer team in my congregation
   ❏ My parents
   ❏ My pastor
   ❏ My youth leader
   ❏ My grandparents
   ❏ My Sunday school teacher
   ❏ Someone special in my congregation
   ❏ My brother/sister
   ❏ My extended family
   ❏ My friends

3. Samuel's parents faithfully repented of their sins. Why was repentance taken so seriously in the Old Testament? How often do you repent of your sins?

4. My parents are committed to passing on the Christian faith to me.

   ❏ I strongly agree.   ❏ I agree.   ❏ I disagree.   ❏ I strongly disagree.

5. *Oh man,* thought James, *here comes Mrs. Kendrick.* He looked around quickly to see if there was any place he could hide. James could get away, but he knew it would be too obvious. She was a nice lady, and he didn't want to hurt her feelings. It was just that after every church service she always seemed to zero in on him and say she was praying for him and knew that God was watching over him. James figured it must be true because he knew that Mrs. Kendrick talked to God a lot.

   Do you have a "Mrs. Kendrick" in your life?

6. How many people do you think you need in your life to help you grow spiritually?

READ OUT LOUD

Today's story looks at the commitment Elkanah and Hannah had to the Lord and to the spiritual growth of their son, Samuel. Elkanah went yearly to a place called Shiloh to worship and sacrifice to God. Shiloh was where the sacred chest, called the Ark of the Covenant, was kept. Elkanah and Hannah took their faith responsibilities seriously. They sought God's forgiveness for themselves and Samuel through their animal and grain sacrifices. They prayed for Samuel. They taught Samuel the Ten Commandments. They insured that Samuel had a spiritual mentor (a priest named Eli). Read the story found in 1 Samuel 1:1-24.

ASK

How many inches did you grow during your last growth spurt?

DISCUSS, BY THE NUMBERS

1. 1 Samuel 1:3 calls God the "Lord Almighty" to distinguish the God of the Bible from the other objects worshiped by those in Samuel's day. At that time many people worshiped angels as well as the planets, moon, sun, and stars. Today's passage tells the reader that the Lord was the maker and ruler of all these things. The point of this activity is to show that many adults don't worship Jesus. Use this as a time to talk about the need for adult mentors who are committed to passing on their faith to this generation. (Note: This is not a time for putting parents down who aren't passing on faith.)

2. Your group members may have never considered the importance of others praying for them. Use this as a time to talk about the benefits of surrounding ourselves with "prayer warriors" willing to dedicate themselves to praying for our spiritual well-being and growth.

3. Samuel's parents faithfully repented of their sins. Why was repentance taken so seriously in the Old Testament? Use this question as an opportunity to talk about the evil that entered the world with Adam and Eve's sin, and how a holy God had to punish sin. Fortunately, God had a remedy named *Jesus Christ.* How often do you repent of your sins?

Repentance is a gift of grace whereby God lets us come before him to say we are sorry for our sins and turn our lives in a new direction. See 1 John 1:9.

4. Use this exercise to talk about how parents are passing on the faith and how your group members need to take advantage of their parents' efforts (even though they may think they are lame). Some of your group members will not have parents committed to passing on the Christian faith. Talk about how they can connect with adults in your congregation who they can look to as role models.

5. Use this true-to-life situation to discuss who the "Mrs. Kendricks" are in your congregation, why they are so important for our Christian growth, and how your group members can attach themselves to them.

6. Listen to the responses of your group members. Share a story from your life about the people who have helped you. When we count them up, we find that there are many people who help us grow spiritually. This means we must be open to letting many people into our lives as spiritual mentors.

THE CLOSE

There are more people than you realize who are committed to your spiritual growth. From our pastor and board members to the volunteers who work with you and the people who tithe so that our congregation can do ministry, you are surrounded by people who want to see your relationship with Christ go deeper and deeper. What will your response be to this circle of caring?

Samuel Gets Called

How is the Lord talking to you?

1. Tradition says that Samuel was a 12-year-old boy when God spoke to him. How old do you think you need to be today so that God will speak to you?

   ❑ Any age
   ❑ Teenage years or older
   ❑ Adulthood

2. Samuel slept near the holy place where God's sacred chest was located. That's probably where God's voice came from. If you were to audibly hear Jesus speak to you, what do you think he would say?

   ❑ You're in big trouble.
   ❑ Why didn't you do your homework?
   ❑ Your mother knows.
   ❑ You're forgiven.
   ❑ Get 'er done.
   ❑ Stop whining.

   ❑ Please talk with your friends about me.
   ❑ I hope we can talk more.
   ❑ Did you hear the one about . . . ?
   ❑ I love you more than you know.
   ❑ It's my voice you need to listen to.
   ❑ What do you think about black holes?

3. How eager are you to hear God speak to you?

   ❑ I don't think I would recognize God's voice.
   ❑ Not really eager
   ❑ Somewhat eager

   ❑ Eager
   ❑ Really eager

4. Finish these sentence stems:

   ❑ God speaks to me through—
   ❑ I listen to God when—
   ❑ I wish the Lord would tell me—

5. On the drive home from church, Elizabeth thought about what the pastor had said during the service—that each of us is "called" to do certain things. That sounded scary to Elizabeth. Most of the stuff he said meant having to talk to other people—you know, like share her faith or help people she didn't know. She just wasn't sure if God wanted her to do that sort of stuff; she kind of hoped not.

   What do you think Elizabeth should do?

READ OUT LOUD

Samuel, a young person in the Old Testament, served the Lord by serving the priest Eli. God spoke directly to Samuel one evening, calling him by name three times. He seemed surprised, thinking it was Eli. Wouldn't you? Samuel grew in his relationship with God as he got older, eventually becoming a prophet in Israel. Read the story out loud from 1 Samuel 3:1-21.

ASK

Who talks with you the most during a typical day?

DISCUSS, BY THE NUMBERS

1. Male Jews were obliged to come before God at the temple in Jerusalem. We see Jesus there when he was 12 (Luke 2:42). Tradition puts Samuel at the age of 12 when God first spoke to him directly. Use this activity to talk about your group members intentionally listening to God at their ages.

2. The original Ten Commandments were kept in the sacred chest. It was the chest where God came to communicate with the priest. It was the chest in which God's glory dwelt. It would not have been unusual for God to speak to Samuel out of this chest. Use this activity to talk about what Jesus might audibly say to your group members. Then discuss how God does communicate to you and your group members through parents, sermons, worship, Scripture, and prayer.

3. Often young people believe that if they could hear or see God, then they would "really believe." Point out that God has spoken through Jesus and through his word, the Bible. God is eager to talk with you and your group members! Are we ready to listen?

4. Listen to the completed sentence stems. Talk together about those times when God has our undivided attention. Ask, "What needs to happen in our lives for God to get our attention?"

5. Use this true-to-life situation to talk together about what God has told your group members. The Scriptures are filled with verses about what God desires of us. God wants us to remain sexually pure (1 Thessalonians 4:3), to live at peace with each other (Romans 12:18), to never stop praying (1 Thessalonians 5:17), and much more.

THE CLOSE

The Lord talks to us and with us in all kinds of ways. We can see how God speaks to us through Scripture, through listening patiently and quietly in prayer, through circumstances, through others, through the Holy Spirit living in us, or through our congregation. The question we must ask ourselves is, "Are we ready to do the work of listening to God?"

God's People Get Conceited

Confidence in religion won't save you

1. Samantha looked at the girl across the lunch table. Somehow they started talking about religion and church and stuff, and this girl said that her church was the "right" church. The girl went on to say that people who went to other churches were being fooled by lies. Who did she think she was anyway? Samantha knew that her church was the "right" one.

   Does going to the "right" church save you?

2. After God's people were defeated in battle, what mistake did they make? (You can check more than one answer.)

   ❏ They took matters into their own hands.
   ❏ They didn't listen to their mothers.
   ❏ They neglected to pray.
   ❏ They didn't get a good night's sleep.
   ❏ They didn't try to find out what God wanted them to do.

   ❏ They rushed off without thinking through their decision.
   ❏ They didn't eat their vegetables.
   ❏ They didn't say they were sorry for their sins.

3. Do you think if you wore a cross necklace that you'd have Jesus' influence with you?

   ❏ Definitely
   ❏ Maybe
   ❏ Not at all

4. God lives in the church building.

   ❏ YES   ❏ NO   ❏ I don't know

5. Andrew's mom loved to watch talk shows in the afternoon. He really didn't pay much attention to them. Today he happened to be in the room when the host said that the topic would be "religious beliefs." She went on to list religions such as Buddhism, Hinduism, New Age, Islam, and Mormonism. Then she said that the guests on the show would be talking about how it wasn't so much what you believe that gets you to heaven but how sincere you are about your belief. Andrew was confused. At church he learned that believing in Jesus was the only way to heaven. Could the TV show host be telling the truth?

   What do you think? Does it matter if you believe in Jesus?

6. What would you say to a non-Christian who believes his or her religion is the only way to God?

   ❏ You're stupid.
   ❏ That's interesting. Let's talk.
   ❏ I guess you're right.

READ OUT LOUD

God's people had again disobeyed the Lord. They worshiped false gods and did what they thought was right. They had come to see the Ark (or sacred chest) containing the Ten Commandments—the place where God's glory resided. Other nations carried their gods into battle, and since Israel wanted to be like these other nations, they took their God-in-a-Box into battle hoping this would give them the victory. Read what happened in 1 Samuel 4:1-11.

ASK

When you were younger, where did you think God lived?

DISCUSS, BY THE NUMBERS

1. Church attendance is never mentioned by Jesus or the Apostles as necessary for salvation. However, church participation is necessary for us to grow in our faith. Jesus invented the church as a community in which we together grow in our faith as we make disciples. No salvation "points" are given by God for attendance—salvation can't be earned—but we do receive great benefits by going to church. As to the "right" church, it is important to go to a church where you can both grow and serve.

2. Instead of repenting and seeking God's will, God's people rushed off and took matters into their own hands. The checked boxes below are statements that answer the question.

   ☑ They took matters into their own hands.
   ❏ They didn't listen to their mothers.
   ☑ They neglected to pray.
   ❏ They didn't get a good night's sleep.
   ☑ They didn't try to find out what God wanted them to do.
   ☑ They rushed off without thinking through their decision.
   ❏ They didn't eat their vegetables.
   ☑ They didn't say they were sorry for their sins.

3. Like the sacred chest, we have sacred objects that can sometimes take the place of God. Ask, "Do we worship religious trinkets, such as crosses around our necks? Christian T-shirts? Christian bumper stickers? Paintings or drawings of Jesus? Movies about Jesus?"

4. Today we often mistakenly refer to our place of worship as a *sanctuary*, which means the dwelling place of God. Just like the Israelites and the Philistines, we tend to believe God lives in a special building. The Bible tells us that God dwells through the Holy Spirit inside our hearts. God is present in our church buildings because we, the people called the church, are there!

5. Use this true-to-life situation as an opportunity to talk about Jesus as the way, the truth, and the life (see John 14:6).

6. Explore what would happen if you called them "stupid" or answered "I guess you're right." Then discuss ways you could develop the relationship and keep talking with the person about what he or she believes and what you believe. Use a real situation from your life or someone you know to describe how this can work.

THE CLOSE

Let's remember that the God-in-a-Box belief only hurt God's people in today's story. God is bigger than any box. We can't categorize God or think we have all the answers to all the questions about God. We know only what God has revealed to us—that Jesus lived, died, and rose again to give us new life. Let's go out from here with a desire to learn more about God through the Bible so that we can live for Jesus each day as we tell others about him and grow in him.

My God Is Bigger

How big is your God?

1. The Philistines wanted to insult God. They put the sacred chest called the Ark in the temple of the Philistine god. How do people try to insult Jesus today?

   - ❏ Make fun of his followers.
   - ❏ Make fun of the Trinity.
   - ❏ Say things like "the church is filled with hypocrites."
   - ❏ Try to get followers of Christ to sin.

2. Dagon fell into a worship position before God's sacred chest. What do you think this proved?

   - ❏ The God of Israel was superior to the god Dagon.
   - ❏ The Philistine night janitor should be more careful when dusting the idols.
   - ❏ Dagon was a false god.
   - ❏ The Philistines were worshiping the wrong deity.
   - ❏ The Lord has a sense of humor.

3. The Philistines continued to worship Dagon even though the Lord demonstrated his superiority. Why do people today refuse to put their trust in Jesus?

   - ❏ They want to do whatever they want to do.
   - ❏ They don't want to admit they are sinners.
   - ❏ They are afraid.
   - ❏ They are losers.
   - ❏ They are stubborn.
   - ❏ They don't like change.
   - ❏ They are comfortable with their beliefs.
   - ❏ They don't want to be thrown out of their families.

4. "Oh my God," Jake said as he watched a car explode on the TV show that he and his dad were watching.
   "Jake," his dad said. "I don't want you saying that."
   "What?" asked Jake. He wasn't trying to be a smart mouth; he really didn't know.
   "I don't want you to use God's name like that," said his father. "It's disrespectful."
   "I never really thought about it that way before," Jake said. Most of Jake's friends say it, and Jake must have just picked it up. He couldn't stop them from using God's name like that—but he didn't have to.

   What do you think of Jake's response to his father?

5. Jesus Christ is a—

   - ❏ fake.
   - ❏ big God who died and rose again for our sins.
   - ❏ god among many gods, like the Mormon church teaches.
   - ❏ great prophet but not God, like the Muslims teach.
   - ❏ part of the oneness of the universe, like New Agers teach.

READ OUT LOUD

The Philistines defeated Israel in a huge battle in which 4,000 Israelites lost their lives. The Philistines took the sacred chest called the Ark of the Covenant as one of the spoils of war. They placed the sacred chest in the temple of Dagon, one of the gods they worshiped. This act of dedicating the spoils of war to Dagon showed their gratitude and proved to the Philistines the power their gods had over the God of Israel. The Philistines were saying to Israel, "Our god is bigger than your God!" What an insult to the God of the Bible. Read the story from 1 Samuel 5:1-12.

ASK

What is the biggest thing in your room?

DISCUSS, BY THE NUMBERS

1. Ask, "Which of the four insults to Jesus have you witnessed?
   - ❏ Make fun of his followers
   - ❏ Make fun of the Trinity
   - ❏ Say things like "the church is filled with hypocrites."
   - ❏ Try to get followers of Christ to sin.
2. See commentary in bold after each statement:
   - The God of Israel was superior to the god Dagon. **This certainly was a demonstration of God's power.**
   - The Philistine night janitor should be more careful when dusting the idols. **It wouldn't have been a good thing for the person who was the temple cleaner. But after blaming the janitor, the Philistine religious leaders would have concluded that the God of the Bible certainly had awesome power.**
   - Dagon was a false god. **While true, the Philistines would have had difficulty abandoning Dagon. That's why God sent further proof in the form of tumors.**
   - The Philistines were worshiping the wrong deity. **Like the previous statement, the Philistines would be wondering if Dagon was the right god to worship.**
   - The Lord has a sense of humor. **It's easy to laugh now at God's sense of humor, but the Philistines were more frightened than humored.**
3. Often people refuse to put their trust in Jesus because they don't want Christ to have a claim on their lives; instead they want to be in charge.
4. Use this true-to-life situation to talk about a specific way that people insult God today—one of which is misusing God's name.
5. This activity helps your group members choose the kind of Jesus they serve. Ask, "If Jesus really did die and came back to life, how then should we live?"

THE CLOSE

Our God is a big God who exists in three persons—Father, Son, and Holy Spirit. This God is big enough to handle your questions and doubts, meet your daily needs, and walk with you through your suffering. This God is the creator of all things—and so this God can handle all of your problems.

1. When are you the most serious about your relationship with Jesus Christ?

- ❑ At school
- ❑ Playing sports
- ❑ At church
- ❑ At camp or a church retreat
- ❑ With one of my parents
- ❑ Alone time
- ❑ Traveling in the car

Another Reminder

We need periodic prompts to stay on track with Jesus

2. Samuel intervened with God for the Israelites. How many people are praying for you?

- ❑ More than 10 people pray for me regularly.
- ❑ Two to 10 people pray for me regularly.
- ❑ One or two people pray for me regularly.
- ❑ No one prays for me regularly.

3. Samuel set up a rock monument called the Stone of Help. This stone was to be a reminder of the victory God gave the Israelites—a prompt of God's goodness and mercy. How often do you need to be reminded of God's goodness and mercy?

- ❑ Every day
- ❑ Every week
- ❑ Once a month or so
- ❑ Hardly ever
- ❑ Never

4. Do you agree or disagree with each of these statements?

Listening to a sermon helps a young person stay on track with Jesus.
❑ I agree. ❑ I disagree.

Worshiping at church helps a young person stay on track with Jesus.
❑ I agree. ❑ I disagree.

Reading the Bible and praying at home helps a young person stay on track with Jesus.
❑ I agree. ❑ I disagree.

Taking communion helps a young person stay on track with Jesus.
❑ I agree. ❑ I disagree.

Going to Sunday school helps a young person stay on track with Jesus.
❑ I agree. ❑ I disagree.

5. "You're going to church again?" Samantha asked her dad. "We just went to church two days ago."
"I know," said her father, "but this is different. This is the Bible study for men from our church."
"But we just studied the Bible on Sunday," Samantha said. "Why do you have to do it again?"
"I don't have to," said her dad. "But sometimes it's nice to take a break during the week and talk about Jesus."
Maybe it's a grownup thing, thought Samantha.

Why do you think Samantha's dad wanted to go to the men's group?

READ OUT LOUD

Today's account takes place over a 20-year period. The sacred chest in which the Ten Commandments were kept, and from which the Lord spoke to the people, was returned from the Philistines. The people of God suffered over the 20 years because of their idol worship. Finally they cried out to the Lord for help. Samuel reminded them of what they needed to do to get right again with God. The Philistine army attacked, and God gave Israel the victory. Read the story out loud from 1 Samuel 7:1-17.

ASK

What do you most need to be reminded of—cleaning your room or doing your homework?

DISCUSS, BY THE NUMBERS

1. It's easy to say we love Jesus; it's quite another to show we do. When the people of God finally cried out to God after 20 years of idolatry, Samuel challenged their devotion to God and told them to get rid of all of their idols. Ask, "Why is God serious about us making him number one?" Explore with your group members if they are more serious about Jesus in some settings and not in others. Ask, "How could you be serious about Jesus in every situation?"

2. Read 1 Samuel 7:5 out loud. Samuel did what is called "intercessory prayer" or praying for others. In the Old Testament are many heroes of our faith who practiced intercessory prayer—Abraham, Moses, Samuel, David, Elijah, Jeremiah, and Daniel. The New Testament shows us Paul and Peter, and of course our Lord, Jesus Christ. God holds some things back waiting for us and others to pray. Here is a chance to talk about the importance of praying for others and having others pray for us.

    > Then Samuel said, "Assemble all Israel at Mizpah, and I will intercede with the LORD for you." (1 Samuel 7:5)

3. Tell a story from your life about how you need regular reminders to stay on track with Jesus. Perhaps it's the weekly sermon, Communion, or your small group that motivates you—a true story about your need for a Stone of Help.

4. Ask, "Which of the activities most reminds you to stay on track with Jesus? Why?"

5. Ask, "How do you think Samantha's dad is being reminded of his relationship with Jesus?" "What are these reminders doing to him?" "How could this happen to Samantha?" "To you?"

THE CLOSE

The prophet Samuel reminded Israel of their history of following and serving the Lord. He challenged God's people to get rid of their idols and return to worshiping God exclusively. He prayed for God's people so that God would deliver them from the Philistines. We need the same kind of reminders—people in our lives, worship, sermons, prayer, and Bible study—to remind us to stay on track with Jesus. Just as Israel got off track, we are liable to go astray, too—and with disastrous results, just as Israel experienced.

1. **Samuel's two sons didn't follow his good example.**

Is a parent or grandparent setting a good example for you?
❏ *For sure* ❏ *Sometimes* ❏ *Not really*

If so, are you following that good example?
❏ *For sure* ❏ *Sometimes* ❏ *Not really*

But his sons did not follow his ways. They turned aside after dishonest gain and accepted bribes and perverted justice. (1 Samuel 8:3)

2. **Samuel immediately asked the Lord what to do. What do you do when you have a concern?**

❏ Always go to God right away
❏ Usually go to God right away
❏ Sometimes go to God right away
❏ Rarely or never go to God right away

But when they said, "Give us a king to lead us," this displeased Samuel; so he prayed to the LORD. (1 Samuel 8:6)

3. **Samuel warned the people of God that a king reigning over them would be bad. Who warned you about bullies? About stranger danger? About smoking? About drinking alcohol? About cheating?**

"Now listen to them; but warn them solemnly and let them know what the king who will reign over them will claim as his rights." (God in 1 Samuel 8:9)

4. **What do you think? T (true) or F (false)**

_____ It's easy to get caught up in the ways of the world.
_____ People my age get tricked into acting like everybody else.
_____ The ways of the world—cheating, lying, rumor-spreading, stealing, disobeying parents—will get you what you want in life.
_____ Following Jesus is not a popular thing to do.
_____ You can act like everybody else and still be a Christian.

But the people refused to listen to Samuel. "No!" they said. "We want a king over us. Then we will be like all the other nations, with a king to lead us and to go out before us and fight our battles." (1 Samuel 8:19-20)

5. **"Did you hear about Heather?" Sandra asked the girls as she sat down at the table in the cafeteria. Patty didn't want to listen, but it was so tempting. Sandra always knew all the gossip around the school, and she wasn't afraid to share it.**
** *I should just leave*, thought Patty. But once Sandra started talking about Heather, Patty couldn't resist listening.**

How is Patty getting caught up in the world?

READ OUT LOUD

Samuel served as both a prophet and judge over Israel. Since the time of Moses, God had appointed prophets to give God's people words from the Lord and judges to serve as warrior leaders and help settle disputes. God was their king while the prophets and judges served as God's representatives. We see at the end of the book of Judges (21:25) that "in those days Israel had no king; everyone did as they saw fit." In other words, God was no longer considered their king because everyone made up their own minds about right and wrong. The people of God were distracted by the world. They wanted what each nation around them had—an earthly king. Read all about it in 1 Samuel 8:1-22.

ASK

What most distracts you from getting your chores done?

DISCUSS, BY THE NUMBERS

1. Read 1 Samuel 8:3. Talk about the examples in the lives of your young people. Ask, "What are your good examples doing right?" "Why do you think some young people reject the good examples set by their parents and grandparents?" "Who else sets good examples for you?" "What kind of example are you setting for those younger than you?"

2. Read 1 Samuel 8:6 out loud. Honestly share where you see yourself. We often try to figure out what we can do to solve a problem or concern before we pray. Talk about how we can practice going to God first.

    But when they said, "Give us a king to lead us," this displeased Samuel; so he prayed to the LORD.
    (1 Samuel 8:6)

3. Read 1 Samuel 8:9 out loud. Talk about who usually warns your group members about risky behaviors. Ask, "Who are you most likely to listen to? Least likely to listen to? Why?"

    "Now listen to them; but warn them solemnly and let them know what the king who will reign over them will claim as his rights."
    (God in 1 Samuel 8:9)

4. Read 1 Samuel 8:19-20 out loud. See commentary in bold after each statement:
   - It's easy to get caught up in the ways of the world. **If we aren't careful, it can be easy.**
   - People my age get tricked into acting like everybody else. **Getting caught up in the world happens subtly.**
   - The ways of the world—cheating, lying, rumor-spreading, stealing, disobeying parents—will get you what you want in life. **It may appear as though these things get you what you want, especially when you see others who're good at it! But the bad consequences outweigh the good. You can tell a story about how you've seen consequences hurt someone who followed the ways of the world.**
   - Following Jesus is not a popular thing to do. **It depends upon the group you're hanging around.**
   - You can act like everybody else and still be a Christian. **Not usually. More often than not being a strong Christian at least means you must go counter to the culture.**

    But the people refused to listen to Samuel. "No!" they said. "We want a king over us. Then we will be like all the other nations, with a king to lead us and to go out before us and fight our battles." (1 Samuel 8:19-20)

5. As a group decide if Patty is or is not getting caught up in the world. Tell a story of how you avoided getting caught up in the world.

THE CLOSE

The Israelites, the people of God, were caught up in the ways of the world. They had begun again to worship false gods. They had rejected the one true God as their Lord and King. God's people had taken matters into their own hands. We, too, can easily do the same. It starts innocently enough at first. We want what others have. Then before we know it, we've pushed God aside. In contrast to the Israelites, Samuel kept God number one in his life. He knew what could happen to him if he turned away from God and wanted no part of it. Today, we have a choice, too: Will we stick with Jesus or get caught up in the world?

God's Imperfect People Get God's Perfect Will

God works in our lives even though we don't follow God as we should

1. God chose Saul and God has chosen you. What are you willing to do for God?

- ❏ I don't want to do anything for God.
- ❏ I'll do something as long as it doesn't cut into my time.
- ❏ I'll do something if I have to.
- ❏ I'll do whatever God wants me to do.

2. "Go say hello," Vanessa's mother whispered to her as they stood in the courtyard after church. "No one else seems to be talking to her."

Vanessa's mom was talking about the new girl in Vanessa's Sunday school class. She looked kind of lonely and lost. But saying hello to new kids just wasn't Vanessa's thing. She was very shy and talking to strangers really put her out of her comfort zone.

But Vanessa remembered that she had prayed for this to happen; that God would put her in situations where she could be used to help others come to Jesus. *Okay, Lord,* Vanessa thought, *I get it. This is one of those opportunities.*

Do you think you should pray that God would put you in situations that help shape specific character traits that God will use to help others?

3. God changed Saul. Jesus is changing me into a different person who is—

- ❏ wealthy.
- ❏ funny.
- ❏ obedient to God.
- ❏ praying more and more each day.
- ❏ selfish.
- ❏ really cool in front of friends.
- ❏ giving and compassionate.
- ❏ ready to party.
- ❏ finding ways to help less-fortunate people.
- ❏ excited about being part of a congregation.

4. God kept working with Israel even though they no longer wanted God to be their ruler.

- ❏ I want Jesus to rule my life only when I'm at church.
- ❏ I want Jesus to rule my life except when I'm at school.
- ❏ I want Jesus to rule my life all the time.

"But you have now rejected your God, who saves you out of all your disasters and calamities. And you have said, 'No, appoint a king over us.'" (1 Samuel 10:19a)

5. What do you think? Y (yes) or N (no)

I'm not always faithful to Jesus. _____
I'm surprised that God is so patient with me. _____
I often forget to confess my sins to God. _____
God is the only one who can save me from my sins. _____

17. GOD'S IMPERFECT PEOPLE GET GOD'S PERFECT WILL—God works in our lives even though we don't follow God as we should *(1 Samuel 10:1-10)*

READ OUT LOUD

God's people, the Israelites, rejected God as their ruler. They told Samuel of their desire for a king like the nations around them. Amazingly, God granted their wish. While God's people weren't following him perfectly, God still worked through their nation and in their lives. That's good news for us, since we aren't perfect, either. Read the account in 1 Samuel 10:1-10.

ASK

In what class do you get perfect grades?

DISCUSS, BY THE NUMBERS

1. Read 1 Samuel 10:1 out loud. God had a plan for Saul to be king. Use this time to explore the possible plans God has for your group members. (You can also read Ephesians 2:10 out loud as a New Testament companion passage that examines God's plans for your group members.)

   Then Samuel took a flask of olive oil and poured it on Saul's head and kissed him, saying, "Has not the LORD anointed you ruler over his inheritance?" (1 Samuel 10:1)

   For we are God's handiwork, created in Christ Jesus to do good works, which God prepared in advance for us to do. (Ephesians 2:10)

2. God doesn't wait until we are perfect before working in our lives. From the moment God gets a hold of us, God is shaping us to be more like Jesus. God will meet us wherever we are but won't keep us there. Talk about the question, "Do you think you should pray for God to put situations in your life to help shape specific character traits to be used to help others?"

3. Read 1 Samuel 10:6 out loud. Like God did in the life of Saul, God is working in you to change you into a new person. Look at the different traits and decide together with your group members what God ought to do in their lives.

   The Spirit of the LORD will come powerfully upon you, and you will prophesy with them; and you will be changed into a different person. (1 Samuel 10:6)

4. Read 1 Samuel 10:19a out loud. Use this activity to talk about how ready your group members are for Jesus to take control of 100 percent of their lives. Discuss the roadblocks that get in the way of releasing control of our lives to Jesus.

   "But you have now rejected your God, who saves you out of all your disasters and calamities. And you have said, 'No, appoint a king over us.'" (1 Samuel 10:19a)

5. Use these statements to talk together about God's complete faithfulness to us in spite of our lack of complete faithfulness to God. Ask, "What does God's faithfulness motivate you to do?"

THE CLOSE

None of us follows Jesus Christ perfectly. We are works in progress—but that's exactly where God wants us. God is molding us every day to be more like Christ. We only need to be willing. Like the Israelites and Saul, we will blow it again and again—but God won't leave us alone. God keeps putting circumstances in our lives and uses the circumstances in which we put ourselves to work in us. Christ certainly makes life exciting.

Saul Gets a Thumbs Down from God

Our sin disappoints our Creator

1. King Saul intentionally disobeyed God.

   When do you act most like King Saul?
   When do you act least like King Saul?

2. Saul made excuses for his sin. How often do people you know make excuses for their sins?

   ❏ All the time
   ❏ Most of the time
   ❏ Sometimes
   ❏ Hardly ever
   ❏ Never

3. Samuel prayed all night for Saul. Who in your life has stopped obeying God, like Saul, and needs hours and hours of prayer?

   ❏ Someone in my family
   ❏ A close friend of mine
   ❏ A friend of my family's
   ❏ A famous person
   ❏ No one I know

4. David made sure that his shirt was buttoned up. He didn't want his mom to see the T-shirt he was wearing underneath it. There was nothing really wrong with the shirt. It didn't have any bad words or anything like that. It was for a band he really liked. David's friend Jeremy had given it to him for his birthday. The problem was that his mom felt that the band's lyrics were inappropriate. She didn't want people to think that David liked the band's message. His mom said he could keep the shirt but couldn't wear it out—but what good was that? *I mean, I don't want to hurt her feelings*, thought David, *but a guy's got to be cool right? If she doesn't see me wearing it, it won't upset her. Everybody wins.*

   What do you think of David's decision?

5. Saul used peer pressure as an excuse for his sin. Why do you suppose others can so easily influence Christians to sin?

   ❏ Peer pressure can be a strong, sinful influence on those who follow (and don't follow) Christ.
   ❏ Christians enjoy sinning.
   ❏ Christians are broken by sin like everyone else.
   ❏ Christians are uneducated.
   ❏ Christians are incredibly stupid.

   Then Saul said to Samuel, "I have sinned. I violated the LORD's command and your instructions. I was afraid of the men and so I gave in to them. Now I beg you, forgive my sin and come back with me, so that I may worship the LORD." (1 Samuel 15:24-25)

READ OUT LOUD

King Saul turned his back on God. Outwardly he appeared religious, but on the inside he relied on himself rather than God. He rationalized and justified his sinful behavior, convinced of his innocence. His repentance wasn't genuine but done to manipulate Samuel and God's favor. Read the story from 1 Samuel 15:1-35.

ASK

What disappoints you the most about your friends?

DISCUSS, BY THE NUMBERS

1. We are all like King Saul in that we are all broken by sin and in need of forgiveness so that we can have a relationship with God, both now and in the life to come. We're unlike Saul if we choose to live holy lives under the guidance of the Holy Spirit. We will sin again and again, but in these cases we need to ask for forgiveness. But we're like Saul if we stubbornly refuse to turn back to God.

2. Use these statements to continue your faith conversation on the importance of genuine repentance that includes a turning from our sin and toward holy living.

3. We often minimize the importance of prayer. You may have heard someone say, "Well, I guess the only thing I can do is pray," as if that's our fallback option. However, the prophet Samuel went to the Lord in prayer all night. Take time within your discussion to pray for those identified as having turned away from God and needing intercessory prayer.

4. In this true-to-life situation, not only will David's mom be hurt, but so will God. Talk about the reasons why God will be hurt, along with why we don't often realize that many of our actions hurt God. Ask, "What would happen if David considered how his decisions may hurt God before considering how they affect his mother?"

5. Read 1 Samuel 15:24-25 out loud. In this situation Saul used others as an excuse for his sin. Use this Bible passage, as well as the activity, to talk about sin and peer pressure.

> Then Saul said to Samuel, "I have sinned. I violated the LORD's command and your instructions. I was afraid of the men and so I gave in to them. Now I beg you, forgive my sin and come back with me, so that I may worship the LORD." (1 Samuel 15:24-25)

THE CLOSE

In case you haven't noticed yet, we live in a world broken by sin. That brokenness applies to us as well. Saul was broken and his sin hurt God; then God disciplined him. This was not punishment. Punishment is reserved for those who are not Christ-followers. Saul was disciplined because his sin let God down. But our sin is no different than Saul's. Let's make a commitment to Christ and turn from our sin. Let's learn from Saul and quit hurting God with our sin.

1. God sent Samuel on a special mission. He hesitated, thinking the mission too dangerous. Why do you hesitate when God wants you to do something, like talk to a friend about Jesus?

❑ I'm unsure it's a mission from God.
❑ I fear what others might think of me.
❑ I wonder if I have the time.
❑ I don't want to get involved.
❑ I'm not sure.

19. 1 Samuel 16:1-13

Outward or Inward?

Is your self-worth from what the world sees or what God sees?

2. God's people were to "consecrate" themselves—or set themselves apart—from their normal routines before a sacrifice was given to the Lord. They would change their clothing, wash in clean water, repent of their sins, and pray. What could you do today to "consecrate" yourself before you attend a worship service at your church?

❑ I could pray.
❑ I could say I'm sorry for my sins.
❑ I could read a verse from the Bible.

❑ I could get to the service on time.
❑ I could have a positive attitude.
❑ I could be more aware of God's presence.

3. Do you think the following statements are T (true) or F (false)?

___ A person's looks are important.
___ Appearance is what God cares about most.
___ Appearance counts so much because that's how you get ahead in life.
___ We get our self-worth from our looks—high self-worth for good-looking people and low self-worth for everybody else.
___ Ugly people are hard to look at.

4. David was not seen as worthy, except by God, to serve as the future king of Israel. How do you think God views Christian young people today?

❑ Like God viewed David.
❑ It depends upon the young person.
❑ Not at all like God viewed David.

5. "But Mom," said Jillian as she walked through the store with her mom, "you don't understand. If I don't get a backpack like the ones the kids have at school, everyone will think I'm a total loser."
   "You and I both know that you aren't a loser, Jillian," said her mother. "A backpack doesn't change that."
   "It does at my school," Jillian said.

   What's right or wrong with her mom's viewpoint?
   What's right or wrong with Jillian's attitude?

READ OUT LOUD

Saul disobeyed the Lord again and again. Then God wanted David to be the future King of Israel. God told the prophet Samuel to go to Bethlehem and anoint a son of Jesse as King. Samuel, just as most people do, looked for the handsomest of Jesse's sons to anoint as King. But God rejected Samuel's choice, instead picking the youngest son, David. God turned the worldly view of self-worth on its head. Read the story found in 1 Samuel 16:1-13.

ASK

Who is the best-looking celebrity today?

DISCUSS, BY THE NUMBERS

1. Samuel was afraid that King Saul would kill him if he found out about Samuel's trip to Bethlehem. But God gave him a cover story so Samuel wouldn't have to lie and could avoid getting killed. Use this situation to talk about times you and your group members have hesitated or been afraid to do something, such as witness for Christ.

2. Preparing our hearts for worship with our congregations is something we seldom do. We just show up. Use this activity to talk about worship preparation. Ask, "What does worship do for your self-worth? Does it help you think more about God and less about yourself? Does it help you realize who God really is?"

3. Do you think the following statements are T (true) or F (false)?

   ____ A person's looks are important. **From a worldly perspective the answer is yes. But from God's point of view, your physical appearance doesn't matter.**

   ____ Appearance is what God cares about most. **Read 1 Samuel 16:7 out loud.**

   ____ Appearance counts so much because that's how you get ahead in life. **Our looks seem to count if we get caught up in the worldly competition for power and wealth. However, the world does for the most part respect character and leadership ability.**

   ____ We get our self-worth from our looks—high self-worth for good-looking people and low self-worth for everybody else. **A worldly perspective informs us that self-worth should be based upon wealth, beauty, power, prestige, and athleticism. The Bible teaches that we derive our worth from our relationship with Christ. God looks on the inside to see our character and our righteousness because of Christ.**

   ____ Ugly people are hard to look at. **Remind your group of Jesus' appearance. The Bible, in Isaiah 53:2, describes what Jesus looked like.**

   But the LORD said to Samuel, "Do not consider his appearance or his height, for I have rejected him. The LORD does not look at the things people look at. People look at the outward appearance, but the LORD looks at the heart." (1 Samuel 16:7)

4. Youth was not respected during Old Testament times. Young people were to be seen and not heard. The view was that they lacked the wisdom and maturity to make good decisions. Ask, "Does this apply today? Do young people have something to contribute to their schools? To their families? To their congregations?"

5. Use this true-to-life situation as a practical example of how Christians should view looks.

THE CLOSE

Samuel identified a person's self-worth by looking on the outside. But God is concerned about the heart—the inside of a person. So where do you get your self-worth? From what the world says is attractive . . . or what God sees as attractive?

1. What enemy giants do you face?

- ❏ A relative
- ❏ A bully
- ❏ Myself
- ❏ A teacher
- ❏ The devil
- ❏ A coach
- ❏ An acquaintance

God Gives David a Big Victory

We're winners because of Jesus

2. David worshiped what he called the living God. The Philistines worshiped many gods.

Worshiping Jesus makes me different than those who worship the gods of other religions (such as the gods of Mormonism or the gods of Hinduism).

❏ I agree.   ❏ I disagree.   ❏ I'm not sure.

Worshiping Jesus makes me better than those who worship no god or other gods.

❏ I agree.   ❏ I disagree.   ❏ I'm not sure.

My friends believe in different gods than Jesus.

❏ I agree.   ❏ I disagree.   ❏ I'm not sure.

3. David trusted completely in the power of the living God while Goliath made fun of the living God. I trust (*completely, mostly, somewhat, not at all*) in Jesus.

Underline one answer.

4. David was given the best equipment of the time to fight Goliath. What do we need to fight our spiritual battles?

- ❏ Nothing special
- ❏ Lots of money in the offering plate at church
- ❏ Spiritual armor
- ❏ An expensive Bible
- ❏ I have no idea.

5. Charlotte's mom was diagnosed with cancer when Charlotte was seven years old. Charlotte remembers people talking in hushed voices, and her mom being tired all the time. People at church would come up to Charlotte and say that they were praying for her mother.

Then Charlotte's mother got the good news. The cancer was gone! Their prayers had been answered. Except now, six years later, her mom's cancer had returned. People kept telling her that she just had to have faith. *Well*, thought Charlotte, *everyone had faith six years ago and now look what's happened.* Charlotte just wasn't sure if she could trust the Lord with something this big.

How is Charlotte's mom a winner with Jesus in spite of the cancer's return?

READ OUT LOUD

In today's story, Israel was at war with the Philistines. Things weren't looking good for God's people. The giant Goliath challenged any soldier in Israel's army to fight him for the outcome of the battle. Fearing personal death and defeat for their army, none of Israel's soldiers dared combat Goliath. Israel's reputation, as well as God's, was on the line. Read the story found in 1 Samuel 17:17-54.

ASK

Who is the tallest, strongest person you know?

DISCUSS, BY THE NUMBERS

1. We may not face physically imposing giants as David faced Goliath, but all of us—Christians and non-Christians alike—face problematic people. Use this activity to identify (without naming names) the major "problem people" in the lives of your group members. Discuss how each of these people is our neighbor and needs our forgiveness, mercy, and love.

2. See commentary in bold after each statement:
   - Worshiping Jesus makes me different than those who worship the gods of other religions (such as the gods of Mormonism or the gods of Hinduism). **Worshiping Jesus makes me different than those who worship the gods of other religions. Jesus is unique. He's the only one who said he's the only way:** *"I am the way and the truth and the life. No one comes to the Father except through me"* **(John 14:6).**
   - Worshiping Jesus makes me better than those who worship no god or other gods. **Christ-followers are broken by sin like everyone else—Christians aren't better, just forgiven.**
   - My friends believe in different gods than Jesus. **That's okay—you may be the person God's looking for to show them Christ. But we also want to be positive influences on friends rather than letting them be negative influences on us.**

3. Identify which of the words (*completely, mostly, somewhat, not at all*) was underlined the most. This will lead your group into a faith conversation about what it means to trust in Jesus.

4. Use this activity to talk about the spiritual armor outlined in Ephesians 6:10-17. Read the passage out loud. This passage gives us an overview of what we need to fight our spiritual battles. Point out that this passage clearly teaches that we will face spiritual battles (see verses 11-14). Talk about each of the six pieces of spiritual battle armor: Truth, God's justification of us, readiness to tell others about Christ, faith, hope of our salvation, Scripture.

5. Use this true-to-life situation to start a faith conversation about how followers of Jesus are winners no matter what happens. Reliance on Christ makes his followers winners by definition.

   For to me, to live is Christ and to die is gain.
   (Philippians 1:21)

THE CLOSE

"Winning with Jesus" sounds like a cliché, but Scripture reinforces that giving our lives to Christ does make us winners, no matter what happens to us. David showed us how a reliance on the living God of the Bible can give us hope and help. We don't serve dead gods like those of the Philistines but a living hope that makes life worth living.

Saul's (and Our) Ironic Jealousy

Your resentment hurts you more than those you resent

1. As King Saul became more interested in himself and less interested in his relationship with God, his anger, jealousy, rage, hatred, and resentment toward David grew. Can you recall a time when you thought more of yourself than your relationship with Jesus?

   ❑ Never happened
   ❑ Happened once
   ❑ Happens sometimes
   ❑ Happens all the time

2. When we feel guilty, sorry, or have regrets, often (but not always) it's because the Holy Spirit is telling us that we've sinned (called *conviction*) and need to get right with God. Have you ever been convicted by the Holy Spirit?

   ❑ Never   ❑ Now and then   ❑ Quite a few times   ❑ All the time

3. Revenge is the best response to feelings of resentment.

   ❑ I strongly agree.   ❑ I agree.   ❑ I disagree.   ❑ I strongly disagree.

4. I let feelings of resentment get the best of me.

   ❑ Always true   ❑ Mostly true   ❑ Sometimes true   ❑ Hardly ever true   ❑ Never true

5. Trevor resented the fact that his mom still thought she could tell him to clean his room. He expressed his resentment by ignoring his mom for the rest of the day. When she said something to him, he pretended to not hear her. He didn't think she even noticed until later that night when his father sat him down and told him to go to bed early and think about what he would say the next day when he apologized to his mother.

   Did Trevor deserve that treatment?

6. I know how to let go of resentment.

   ❑ Yes   ❑ No   ❑ I don't know

READ OUT LOUD

King Saul was jealous of David's popularity with the people of Israel. His resentment grew so much so that he sent David into battle to try to get him killed. Today's Bible reading does not follow in strict chronological order, but it does record Saul's resentment toward David. Read the story found in 1 Samuel 18:5-30.

ASK

What is your definition of *resentment*?

DISCUSS, BY THE NUMBERS

1. Ask, "Why do you think it's difficult to be resentful of others when you're focused on your relationship with Christ?" King Saul's relationship with God had deteriorated. The more Saul took charge of his own life and decisions, the more he blocked God out. The result of thinking more about self and less about God was anger, jealousy, rage, hatred, and resentment toward David whom God was blessing. If Saul would have focused on his relationship with God rather than worrying about David's successes, he would have rejoiced for David.

2. The Bible says a tormenting spirit grabbed hold of Saul that made him act crazy (see 1 Samuel 18:10-11). This was probably the Holy Spirit impressing upon Saul a sense of guilt for his sin against God (known as *conviction*). It can be difficult for your group members to personalize conviction to themselves because that requires admitting sin. Begin by telling a story of a time when you felt convicted by the Holy Spirit. How did you respond? Point out that the more we commit a sin (e.g., cheating), the less we feel convicted about our actions because we become desensitized and start viewing our actions as normal. It's during these times that God has to discipline us to bring us back.

3. Revenge is often our default response to feelings of resentment, even if it's only in our heads. But the Bible teaches us that revenge belongs to God (see Leviticus 19:18; Romans 12:19). Ask, "Why do we think revenge will help ease our feelings of resentment? How can revenge make our resentment worse?"

4. Use this activity to talk about how holding on to resentment will eat at you. Resentment can be emotionally debilitating and spiritually crippling because you become preoccupied with it.

5. Use this true-to-life situation to talk about real-life situations that involve resentment. Your group members will come up with other stories. Use these to talk about the consequences of resentment.

6. Here's a five-step process for letting go of resentment. Step #1: Name the resentment (*I feel hurt because Amanda dropped me as a friend*). Step #2: Write a letter addressed to the person describing your resentment. Step #3: Give the resentment to Jesus in prayer by holding the letter up toward heaven. Tear the letter up and throw it away. Step #4: Deliberately choose to look at the person you resent through God's eyes (*Amanda is a broken person who wants to be popular*). Step #5: If the resentment returns, keep giving it to Jesus.

THE CLOSE

Resentment happens because we live in a fallen, broken world filled with fallen, broken people—including you and me. We feel bad when others hurt us. We get angry. Perhaps we rage. We want to get back at them. And we let resentment fester inside us. But guess who is *not* worried about your resentment: The person you resent! So let's give our resentments to God, forgive those we resent, and move on with our lives.

First Things First

Put Jesus in the center of your life

1. What do you think—yes or no?

___ Does your music interfere with putting Jesus in the center of your life?

___ Does your gaming activity interfere with putting Jesus in the center of your life?

___ Does your TV/movie viewing interfere with putting Jesus in the center of your life?

___ Does your social life interfere with putting Jesus in the center of your life?

___ Does your sports life interfere with putting Jesus in the center of your life?

2. Do you think it was fair for God to kill Uzzah?

❏ Yes   ❏ No   ❏ I don't know

3. King David was afraid of God after Uzzah's death. He experienced the consequences of neglecting the sacred chest. How often do you neglect your relationship with Jesus?

❏ All the time   ❏ Most of the time   ❏ Sometimes   ❏ Hardly ever   ❏ Never

4. What do you think?

Families who put Jesus at the center of their family life enjoy each other more.
❏ Always true   ❏ Mostly true   ❏ Sometimes true   ❏ Never true

Families who put Jesus at the center of their family respect each other less.
❏ Always true   ❏ Mostly true   ❏ Sometimes true   ❏ Never true

Families who put Jesus at the center of their family life are more anxious.
❏ Always true   ❏ Mostly true   ❏ Sometimes true   ❏ Never true

Families who put Jesus at the center of their family life are more compassionate.
❏ Always true   ❏ Mostly true   ❏ Sometimes true   ❏ Never true

Families who put Jesus at the center of their family life are not focused on worldly things.
❏ Always true   ❏ Mostly true   ❏ Sometimes true   ❏ Never true

5. Monica rolled her eyes as her family stood by the front door.
   "I saw that," said her dad laughing.
   They were gathered at the front door to pray together like they did almost every day. Even though Monica gave her dad a rough time about it, she really didn't mind. She and her little sister had grown up doing this. Her mom and dad felt that it was important that they start their day by putting Jesus first. They did this by praying together before they went to school and work. Monica usually acted like it was a pain, just to bug her dad, but she knew the day wouldn't feel right if they didn't do it.

   What's the difference between putting Jesus in the center of your life and putting Jesus first?
   How do you put Jesus at the center of your life? Not a to-do list with Jesus at the top and then you moving to the next item on the list—but Jesus in the middle of it all.

READ OUT LOUD

The sacred chest called the Ark of the Covenant was noticeably absent and neglected in the life of Israel for many years. This sacred chest, where the original Ten Commandments were kept, was one of the ways in which God communicated to Israel. It had been stored in a home until David, now King, wanted it brought to Jerusalem to again have a prominent place in the worship of the Lord. King David wanted to put God first. Read the story found in 2 Samuel 6:1-12.

ASK

What happens when you put school first?

DISCUSS, BY THE NUMBERS

1. King David, in his wish to put God first, didn't want any disruptions to interfere with his goal. Use this activity to talk about the things that most interfere with or disrupt your group members from putting God at the center of their lives.

2. A grave mistake was made in the removal of the sacred chest. It was placed on a cart instead of carried on the priests' shoulders as commanded by God (see Numbers 4:15; 7:9; 18:3). They treated the sacred chest like a common object rather than the dwelling place of God's glory on earth. Even though the cart was new, this method of transport was a violation of God's direct command. God required that God's people take God's commands seriously. How serious is God about wanting people to obey him today?

3. King David experienced the consequences of neglecting the sacred chest. God's commands for not taking care of it were clearly spelled out. And we do the same thing as David did—we neglect our relationships with Jesus. Together identify neglected areas (e.g., prayer, Bible reading, worship, service to others), then talk about how you and your group members can make practical changes.

4. There are benefits to putting Jesus at the center of your family life. Talk together about how your group members can be part of putting and keeping Jesus at the center of their family lives. Be especially sensitive to group members whose parents (one or both) aren't followers of Christ. Discuss how these group members can still keep Jesus at the center of their personal lives and let their actions be a witness to their parents.

5. Use this true-to-life situation to get a faith conversation going about the difference between putting Jesus in the center of your life and putting Jesus first.

   Put the following checklist on a whiteboard or chalkboard:

   ___ #1 Jesus
   ___ #2 Family
   ___ #3 School/Work
   ___ #4 Sports practice
   ___ #5 Homework
   ___ #6 Games/Internet

   Say something like, "If you put Jesus at the top of a checklist, he becomes something to check off your list as you go to the next item. Instead let's put Jesus in the center of the circle. This makes Jesus at the center of all we do."

THE CLOSE

Let's do more than simply put Jesus first on a list of things to do. Like King David, let's put Jesus at the center of our lives, at the center of who we are and all we do.

David Listens to God

Open your ears to Christ's voice every day

1. I don't understand what people mean when they say God "spoke" to them.

   ❑ I agree.
   ❑ I disagree.
   ❑ I don't care.

2. Like in King David's life, God speaks to me—

   ❑ Often
   ❑ Sometimes
   ❑ Rarely
   ❑ Never

3. Circle the one word that best describes your prayer life.

   Nonexistent   Dull   Regular   Rare   Weak   Satisfactory   Terrible   Awesome

4. How do you pray?

   ❑ Like I'm talking to a friend
   ❑ Like I'm sending a text
   ❑ Like I'm speaking to a parent
   ❑ Like I have a good relationship with God
   ❑ Like I'm pleading with God
   ❑ Like I'm bothering God

5. "Is that like listening to the voices in my head?" Todd asked with a laugh. He was always the comedian in Sunday school class. It was funny at first, but then it got annoying. Today the teacher was talking about listening for God's voice. Todd couldn't help himself. It just sounded too weird. Who walks around listening for God? How do you hear God anyway?
   "Is he talking now?" asked Todd, cupping his hand to his ear. "I can't hear him."

   Why do you suppose some non-believers react to prayer like Todd?
   How is prayer beneficial in your life?

READ OUT LOUD

The prophet Nathan spoke for God to God's people in Israel. Somehow God spoke directly to him and then asked Nathan to deliver the message to the nation—or in this case, to the nation's King. David received the Lord's message attentively then went to the tent where the sacred chest (the Ark of the Covenant) was kept and prayed. Read the story found in 2 Samuel 7:1-22.

ASK

Who do you listen to the most?

DISCUSS, BY THE NUMBERS

1. This question can get a faith conversation going about how God speaks to us today. First, allow your group members to talk about confusion regarding the ways they believe or don't believe God speaks to them. Item #2 will help you explore specific ways God does speak with you and your group members.

2. David heard God through the prophet Nathan. We can hear God's voice through sermons, worship songs, Bible studies with others, personal Bible study, or contemplative prayer. The distractions of TV and movies, busyness, friends, or sports can block the voice of God.

3. Use this activity as a springboard to talk about—
   - Prayer Position: While position doesn't necessarily matter, kneeling, bowing, or lying prostrate on the floor can help humble us before God so that we are more prepared to talk and listen.
   - Prayer Time: Encourage your group members to extend the time they pray. If they are praying once each day now, ask them if they could pray twice. If they pray for four minutes now, ask them to double that to eight minutes.
   - Prayer Place: A regular place like the bedroom or while jogging along the river can assist us in remembering to pray as well as quieting our minds to pray and listen for God's voice.

4. See commentary in bold after each statement:
   - Like I'm talking to a friend. **We can talk with God as friends because we are (see John 15:15).**
   - Like I'm sending a text. **While we can shoot up an arrow prayer when we are in the middle of something, we must make time for longer prayers.**
   - Like I'm speaking to a parent. **God is not a punitive God waiting to punish us for our wrongdoings, but a compassionate God who wants to hear our concerns, our praises, and our thanks.**
   - Like I have a good relationship with God. **Because of Christ we can have a great relationship with God. We need only confess our sins to Christ and believe that through him we have eternal life—then we can approach God boldly (see Hebrews 4:16).**
   - Like I'm pleading with God. S**ometimes we do plead with God. King David in the Old Testament certainly did. God wants to hear from us, even our pleadings.**
   - Like I'm bothering God. **When we pray to a god who is bothered by our prayers, we are praying to a small god. But God is big—and has time for us, night and day.**

5. Use this true-to-life situation to discuss the absurdity of prayer from a worldly perspective, and the necessity and benefits of prayer from a Christian perspective.

THE CLOSE

The voice of God can be heard in all kinds of places—but we must be willing to hear it. God can speak directly to us through the nudging of the Holy Spirit as we read the Bible, listen to a sermon, take a hike in the wilderness, or participate in a small group Bible study. Ask, "Are you ready to practice listening to God?"

1. **How can you be kind to your friends like David was kind to Jonathan and Mephibosheth?**

   ❑ Comforting them when they are sad
   ❑ Doing everything they ask you to do
   ❑ Lying for them
   ❑ Keeping their secrets
   ❑ Spending time with them
   ❑ Being mean to your friend's enemies
   ❑ Getting them gifts for their birthdays
   ❑ Helping them with their homework
   ❑ Sharing with them
   ❑ Encouraging them when they are down

2. **Mephibosheth was only five when his father, Jonathan, died. Mephibosheth now had his own son. David obviously took years to fulfill the friendship promise he made to Jonathan. When it comes to keeping my promises to my friends, I . . .**

   ❑ Always keep them.   ❑ Usually keep them.
   ❑ Mostly keep them.   ❑ Never keep them.

3. **How do you usually handle interactions with those who are disabled?**

   ❑ I treat them like anyone else.   ❑ I try to get to know them.
   ❑ I make fun of them.   ❑ I ignore them.
   ❑ I treat them like they're weird.

4. **What does it feel like to receive kindness from someone, like David gave to Mephibosheth?**

   ❑ I don't deserve it.   ❑ I don't expect it in today's world.
   ❑ I like the attention.   ❑ I repay their kindness.
   ❑ I should always be treated well.

5. **Since Grandpa got sick a few months ago, Ben's family had been visiting him every week. Ben knew his grandpa really looked forward to those visits. Ben loved his grandpa, but he didn't enjoy visiting him. His grandpa and the other people in the nursing home looked weird and smelled funny. Some of them couldn't talk very well because they had what his mom called a "stroke." Some of them were in wheelchairs, and some just lay in their beds. It was creepy. How could he tell his mom that he didn't want to go back again?**

   What do you think of Ben's attitude? Is this how Jesus would view the situation?

READ OUT LOUD

King Saul and his son Jonathan, who was King David's best friend, were both dead. David wanted to honor his friend, so he asked about Jonathan's family. He learned that Jonathan's son, Mephibosheth, was alive. At five years old his legs were injured by the neglect of a nurse. David had never met Mephibosheth, but David wanted to show him kindness because of the friendship David had with his father. Read the story found in 2 Samuel 9:1-13.

ASK

Have you ever stared at a disabled person?

DISCUSS, BY THE NUMBERS

1. Use this activity to discuss the importance of true friends. Ask, "How many Christian friends and non-Christian friends should a Christian have?" "Do you have any friends for whom you would be willing to take care of their future children?"

2. Jonathan and David had such a close friendship that they promised to look out for each other's children if something ever happened to either of them. Read 1 Samuel 20:14-17 out loud. Use this passage to discuss the attributes of a friendship that "*shows unfailing kindness like the Lord's kindness.*"

   But show me [Jonathan] unfailing kindness like the LORD's kindness as long as I live, so that I may not be killed, and do not ever cut off your kindness from my family—not even when the LORD has cut off every one of David's enemies from the face of the earth." So Jonathan made a covenant with the house of David, saying, "May the LORD call David's enemies to account." And Jonathan had David reaffirm his oath out of love for him, because he loved him as he loved himself. (1 Samuel 20:14-17)

3. See commentary in bold after each statement:
   - I treat them like anyone else. **People often pity disabled people—but typically those with disabilities want to be treated like everyone else and stay as independent as possible. So do that for them!**
   - I make fun of them. **In biblical times those with disabilities were viewed as sinners who de-** served their infirmities. But in John 9:2 Jesus was asked if a blind man's parents—or the man's sin—caused his blindness; Jesus said neither. Bad stuff happens because we live in a sinful world. Ask your group to remember times when they were ridiculed or judged. Were they pleasant experiences? Then don't treat others like that!
   - I treat them like they're weird. **First, ask the group to define *weird*. Then ask, "How weird are people without disabilities?" The point is to show that sin has broken all of us—and we're all weird in our own way. Christians are commanded to love everyone, including "enemies" (which includes "weird" people).**
   - I try to get to know them. **When you get to know those with disabilities, you'll find they're human like everyone else, sinners like everyone else, and need Jesus just like everyone else.**
   - I ignore them. **By showing love to them, we show the love of Christ to the world.**

4. The point of this activity is to show that David and Jonathan, as true friends, understood that we live in community. The church is a community of faith. Jesus established the church so that we could live together and support each other as we bring God's kingdom into this world. It takes a community called the church to share the good news of Jesus.

5. Use this true-to-life situation to explore similar life stories your young people have experienced.

THE CLOSE

Jesus' heart was with the sick, the poor, the outcast, the homeless, and yes, the disabled. Read what Jesus said from Mark 2:17. Jesus was interested in those who knew they were broken, not those who thought they were already "healthy."

> *On hearing this, Jesus said to them, "It is not the healthy who need a doctor, but the sick. I have not come to call the righteous, but sinners."*
> *(Jesus in Mark 2:17)*

1. **What was the first "sin" that you felt guilty about committing?**

   - ❏ Breaking a toy and not telling your parents
   - ❏ Lying about being sick
   - ❏ Fighting with your siblings and calling them names
   - ❏ Disobeying your parents
   - ❏ Copying someone else's schoolwork

2. **Check the boxes that you agree with:**

   - ❏ My sin hurts only me.
   - ❏ *Sin* is a word used only to make people feel bad about their actions.
   - ❏ I've never committed a really big sin.
   - ❏ I don't think about my sins.
   - ❏ After I sin I'm too ashamed to talk to God for a while.
   - ❏ I could stop sinning if I wanted to.
   - ❏ My friends tempt me to sin.

3. **Why do you think David tried to cover up his initial sin (of sleeping with Bathsheba) with even more sin (like lying and murder)?**

   - ❏ He was trying to cover up his next mistakes.
   - ❏ He thought he could hide his faults from God.
   - ❏ He already sinned once—why not a few more times?
   - ❏ He was embarrassed.
   - ❏ It was easier to keep sinning than face the consequences.

4. **Finish this sentence:**

   After I sin, I feel—

5. **Choose two sins you're struggling with right now from the list below. (You don't have to check these or talk about them.)**

   - ❏ Lying   ❏ Lust   ❏ Gossip   ❏ Cheating   ❏ Bullying   Jealousy
   - ❏ Greed   ❏ Envy   ❏ Stealing   ❏ Other_____

6. Her dad said she had a "smart mouth." Her mom said she needed to stop back-talking. Her parents usually grounded her after telling her these things. Her teachers sent her to the office with referrals for detention. You'd think Connie would've learned by now not to speak disrespectfully to adults, but she didn't—other kids thought she was funny and brave for saying the things she did. Now most of the time the words were out of her mouth before she could stop them—and the consequences were getting bigger, too.

   How difficult will it be for Connie to stop?

(2 Samuel 11:1-27)

READ OUT LOUD

What a story! King David was tempted by pleasure that he wasn't meant to take part in, but he didn't turn away—instead he gave in. Then when the consequences struck, King David decided to try covering up his initial sin with more sin. David could have walked away from his first temptation and avoided the sin as well as the cover up (or at least the cover up). But he didn't. Read the account found in 2 Samuel 11:1-27.

ASK

Have you ever told a lie to cover up another lie?

DISCUSS, BY THE NUMBERS

1. Use this activity to discuss how common sin is in our world. We begin sinning as children and struggle with sin all our lives.
2. See commentary in bold after each statement:
   - My sin hurts only me. **Sin hurts God, your congregation, your friendships, as well as the person or people you sinned against.**
   - *Sin* is a word used only to make people feel bad about their actions. ***Sin* is a word not often used in our secular culture. The world doesn't want to be held accountable for its immoral actions. Yet sin is a reality in our world—and we are accountable to God for our sin.**
   - I've never committed a really big sin. **All sins are bad, whether we view them as "big" or "little." That's part of the problem—we try to rank them. That's not our job.**
   - I don't think about my sins. **We can become numb to our sins to the point where we don't think much about them anymore. But if we're growing in our relationships with Christ, this won't happen.**
   - After I sin I'm too ashamed to talk to God for a while. **We can immediately go to God when we sin and ask for forgiveness (see 1 John 1:9).**
   - I could stop sinning if I wanted to. **Many sins turn into habits that are difficult to break. It takes conscious and intentional efforts to repent of and end our habitual sinning.**
   - My friends tempt me to sin. **Talk about being an influencer to do right rather than someone who's always influenced to do wrong.**
3. Use this example to discuss how sin can spiral out of control once we give in to temptation.
4. Listen to the completed sentences. Talk about how feeling bad after sinning helps motivate us to repent and change our behaviors. We don't have to keep feeling bad if we repent and make amends (i.e., ask forgiveness of God as well as those we've hurt) for what we've done wrong.
5. Together create a list of strategies for walking away from these sins (see suggestions below). Then decide which strategy or strategies your group thinks could work the best.
   - Pray about it.
   - Surrender that sin to Jesus.
   - Know what situations will tempt you toward that sin—then avoid them.
   - Find friends who don't pressure or tempt you to sin.
   - Talk with someone you trust about what you're going through.
   - Ask a friend to hold you accountable.
6. Use this true-to-life situation as a springboard to discuss similar situations your group members are facing.

THE CLOSE

Sin. It's everywhere. Our world is broken by sin and its consequences, and sin's influence is all over the place. Yet Christians *can* say no to sin—because the Holy Spirit who resides in believers already empowers them to say NO. What did we learn from King David? First he didn't walk away from the temptation. Then he gave in to the temptation and sinned. Then he covered up his sin with more sin. What started out as a look turned into adultery and eventually murder. David could have said NO when the temptation presented itself and walked away. No terrible consequences. No angry God. But he didn't. We can learn from David's errors and lean on the Holy Spirit—and say NO!

Wake-Up Call

To whom are you accountable?

1. What does it mean to be "accountable"?

- ☐ Apologize for lying.
- ☐ Follow through on commitments.
- ☐ Get away with cheating again and again.
- ☐ Go to prison for a crime.
- ☐ Have lenient parents.
- ☐ Teachers buy your excuse for not doing your homework.
- ☐ Get disciplined by parents for a wrongdoing.
- ☐ Get a bad grade on a test as a result of not studying.
- ☐ Go to detention for acting out at school.
- ☐ Other: _____

2. What do you think the world would look like if people were never held accountable for their actions?

- ☐ More fun than it is now.
- ☐ Young people would get into a lot less trouble.
- ☐ There would be more crime, including murder.
- ☐ People would be happier.
- ☐ There would be much more poverty.
- ☐ Wars would break out all over.
- ☐ Students would learn more in school.

3. To whom are you accountable in your own life?

- ☐ Jesus
- ☐ Friends
- ☐ Employer
- ☐ Sports team
- ☐ Parents
- ☐ Siblings
- ☐ Boyfriend/Girlfriend
- ☐ Coaches
- ☐ Teachers
- ☐ Police
- ☐ Congregation
- ☐ Youth group
- ☐ Neighbors
- ☐ Myself
- ☐ President of the U.S
- ☐ My pet

4. Nathan told the story in 2 Samuel so that—(you can check more than one answer)

- ☐ David could learn about lambs.
- ☐ David could see how it related to his situation.
- ☐ David could learn to become accountable.
- ☐ David would get in trouble with God.
- ☐ David could see that God was hurt by David's sin.

5. Finish this sentence:

God was right to discipline David because—

6. Agree (A) or Disagree (D)

- ___ I always learn when I get disciplined.
- ___ I wish I could get away with more things.
- ___ Accountability is not important to me.
- ___ I hold my friends accountable.
- ___ God only holds me accountable for really big sins.

READ OUT LOUD

You may remember that King David blew it big time. He committed adultery with Bathsheba, and then when she became pregnant with David's child, David had her husband, Uriah, murdered—along with those serving in the army around him. So God sent Nathan, the prophet, as a wake-up call for David. What David tried to do in secret God knew plain as day. God held David accountable—and made David accountable to Nathan and the Israelites. Are we accountable to God and to others? Read the story in 2 Samuel 12:1-10.

ASK

When was the last time you got caught with your hand in the cookie jar?

DISCUSS, BY THE NUMBERS

1. Being "accountable" means answering to someone for your actions. As a group choose those statements that represent an example of being accountable.
2. While we don't usually want to be held accountable, a world without accountability would be a world in chaos—much worse than it is today. Accountability puts the brakes on sin. While sin still occurs frequently, accountability makes people think twice before they do something wrong.
3. Your group members may be surprised to learn how many individuals and groups to which they are accountable. We need so much accountability because we (and everybody else) are wired to sin. We should want accountability because it keeps us honest with ourselves, others, and God.
4. See commentary in bold after each statement:
   - David could learn about lambs. **He was a shepherd as a young boy so he already knew much about lambs.**
   - David could see how it related to his situation. **The story was a magnificent teaching tool because David clearly saw his sin and its consequences on others.**
   - David could learn to become accountable. **David used his authority as king to do an awful thing. The story helped him learn that even as king, he was not above God's laws. We (who aren't even kings or queens) need to learn the same thing.**
   - David would get in trouble with God. **David was already in trouble with God for his sin.**
   - David could see that God was hurt by David's sin. **The story revealed to David how God was hurt by David's sin. Ask, "How often do we consider that our sin might hurt God?"**
5. Listen to the completed sentences, then talk about the need for accountability in our own lives—not just in the lives of those who don't follow Christ.
6. See commentary in bold after each statement:
   - I always learn when I get disciplined. **We don't always learn. Sometimes we pout or get angry because we got caught.**
   - I wish I could get away with more things. **Some of us rebel against God, parents, coaches, teachers, and other authority figures by trying harder to avoid getting caught rather than changing our behaviors. Ask, "What does it take to change our behaviors and learn after being held accountable?"**
   - Accountability is not important to me. **We want others to be held accountable but often wish we didn't have to be held accountable.**
   - I hold my friends accountable. **Usually this is true when it comes to the relationship they have with us.**
   - God only holds me accountable for really big sins. **God holds us accountable for every sin we commit whether or not we get caught by fellow humans.**

THE CLOSE

We are all accountable to God and to others. God held King David accountable for his actions, and God holds us accountable as well. God is also compassionate and doesn't hold our sins against us when we repent and trust in Christ. God is a merciful God who disciplines us when we need it but stands ready to forgive and remember our sins no more when we ask.

David Is Broken

Repentance means more than saying you're sorry

1. When was the last time you "repented" to God for something you did wrong?

- ❏ I have no idea what it means to repent.
- ❏ I haven't committed any big sins, so I don't need to repent.
- ❏ As long as I don't get caught, I don't need to repent.
- ❏ I can't remember.
- ❏ I repent every time I sin.

2. Why do you think God chose to take David's child? (You can choose more than one answer.)

- ❏ God is mean.
- ❏ There are consequences for sin.
- ❏ David's repentance wasn't sincere enough.
- ❏ God knows what's best.
- ❏ We will never know the details this side of heaven.

3. When you sin against the Lord, how do you feel?

- ❏ Ashamed
- ❏ Regretful
- ❏ Nothing
- ❏ Nervous
- ❏ Guilty
- ❏ Sinful
- ❏ Sad
- ❏ Other_____

4. What do you do when you repent?

- ❏ Pray
- ❏ Cry
- ❏ Ask God for forgiveness
- ❏ Plead
- ❏ Go to church
- ❏ Do good works
- ❏ Promise God to never do anything bad again
- ❏ Vow never to get caught again

5. Seth knew it was wrong the moment the words left his mouth. He'd never talked back to his mom before, and he rarely ever swore. To do both to his mom was a shock for both of them. He said he was sorry as soon as he said it. He could tell that she was really hurt, and he wished there was a way he could go back in time and take the words back. Seth told her how sorry he was, and when she hugged him and said she forgave him, he felt a little better—but Seth knew he'd have to make some changes. He really needed to stop hanging around kids at school who swore so much. He also needed to make sure he watched how he talked to his mom.

What do you think Seth needs to do differently?

READ OUT LOUD

Written by David, Psalm 51 records David's response to his sin of murder and adultery. David was a broken man after the prophet Nathan confronted him with his sin. Nathan left David alone with God to repent of his sin. Read the story from 2 Samuel 12:14-23.

ASK

Do you think about sinning after you have been caught in a sin?

DISCUSS, BY THE NUMBERS

1. The word *repent* in Greek is "metanoeo," which means to change your mind. *Meta* means "with"; *noeo* means "understanding." The word then literally means to change your mind based on your understanding. Therefore when we truly repent, we change the way we think about something. It's as if you're driving in one direction when you suddenly realize you are headed the wrong way—and you make a U-turn because the place you want to go is behind you, not in front of you. When we repent, God gives us a second chance, as we're now headed in a new direction.

2. See commentary in bold after each statement:

   • God is mean. **It doesn't seem fair that God took the life of David's baby, but we must trust that God had the ultimate and overall best in mind.**

   • There are consequences for sin. **Yes. Emotional pain is one of them.**

   • David's repentance wasn't sincere enough. **When you read Psalm 51, you see that David sincerely repented of his wrongdoing.**

   • God knows what's best. **God is good all the time. Our sinful nature times the nearly seven billion people in the world can make it seem as though God is unfair and doesn't care what's best for us. But God does know—and God also has given us free will, and that free will is responsible for much of the evil in the world.**

   • We will never know the details this side of heaven. **The full meaning of what happened will not be understood in this life.**

3. Our God-given consciences allow us to feel bad for our wrongdoing. It's an alarm that tells us what we're doing is wrong. Combined with the conviction of the Holy Spirit, we will feel wrong and yucky when we sin. Unfortunately we can train our consciences to feel less bad, allowing us to make sin a habit and ignore God's (and others') feelings.

4. Use these to jumpstart a dialogue on what Christian repentance should look like—a turning around of our behavior.

5. Use this true-to-life situation to explore real-life situations experienced by your group members.

THE CLOSE

Repentance means more than saying you're sorry. Repentance means recognizing that your life is going in the wrong direction—and that a U-turn in thinking and acting is required. David learned this the hard way. He lost a child because of his sin. Can we learn from David's life? Can we see that repentance is necessary for our growth as Christians? Can we turn our lives around before we get ourselves into predicaments as bad as David's?

David's Advice to Solomon

"Walk with Jesus" is the best advice you could ever take

1. What was the name of a pet you loved who died or got lost?

2. What does the Lord require of you?

- ❑ Become an expert at your favorite video game.
- ❑ Attend every church function.
- ❑ Make friends with all the "weird" kids at your school.
- ❑ Go pro in the sport of your choice.
- ❑ Read the whole Bible every year on your own.
- ❑ Fast once each week.
- ❑ Keep a prayer journal.
- ❑ Listen only to Christian music.
- ❑ Pray for an hour each morning.
- ❑ Get straight As in school.

3. King David thought Solomon would do well if he walked in obedience to God. Do you believe this is true today—that we will do well if we follow Christ?

❑ I strongly agree.   ❑ I agree.   ❑ I'm not sure.   ❑ I disagree.   ❑ I strongly disagree.

4. Which of the following statements about Psalm 72:1-20 are true (T) and which are false (F)?

___ King David's prayer for Solomon was selfish.
___ You get hurt only if you're honest and fair.
___ You can't make any money defending the poor.
___ The people of God must help those who are weak and helpless.
___ We should pray for our rulers.

5. Laurie hadn't been raised in a Christian home. In fact, she hadn't been raised in much of a home at all. Her dad left a few years ago, and she hasn't heard from him since; her mom just sort of keeps to herself. It's been pretty lonely. But for the last few months Laurie's friend Cassie invited Laurie over for weekends. It was really fun to be included in the activities of Cassie's family. One of them was church on Sunday morning. Laurie's parents had always made fun of people who went to church, so Laurie was pretty skeptical at first. But Cassie's dad challenged Laurie to check things out for herself and gave her a Bible to read. He told her some of his favorite passages that talked about Jesus' love. Though Laurie's parents' comments kept coming back to her, she found herself reading the Bible more and asking more questions. *My parents must not have known much about Jesus,* she thought, *or they wouldn't have made fun of people who believe in him.*

What do you think happened to get Laurie to change her mind about Jesus?
What advice should Cassie give her friend?

READ OUT LOUD

King David was dying. He gave his throne to his son, Solomon. He advised Solomon to obey the Lord so that he will prosper. He also prayed for Solomon. This prayer was probably the last Psalm that David wrote. Read David's advice to Solomon from 1 Kings 2:1-3 and David's prayer to God for Solomon in Psalm 72:1-20.

ASK

What advice has a parent given you?

DISCUSS, BY THE NUMBERS

1. Use this question, "What was the name of a pet you loved who died or got lost?" as a lead-in to discuss King David's preparation for his own death. David was prepared to die. Death is inevitable whether or not we are prepared, but David made peace with God. He admitted his brokenness. He was forgiven. But many today are not spiritually ready to die. Use these questions to start a faith conversation on why King David was ready to die and who is and is not ready to die today.

2. Read 1 Kings 2:1-3 out loud. Use the list of "extremes" to talk about what the Lord reasonably requires of your group members. See questions in bold after each statement:

   • Become an expert at your favorite video game. **Expertise requires lots of time. Is that what God wants? Or does God want you to balance work in school with a little fun?**

   • Attend every church function. **How many functions does God want you to reasonably attend for personal growth and others' growth?**

   • Make friends with all the "weird" kids at your school. **How many socially disenfranchised friends does God want you to have?**

   • Go pro in the sport of your choice. **This could honor the Lord. Is it a realistic goal, or are there better goals for you to set?**

   • Read the whole Bible every year on your own. **How often should you read the Bible? What parts of the Bible should you read? Where should you start?**

• Fast once each week. **Do you need to fast? What other strategies would help you focus your life more on Jesus?**

• Keep a prayer journal. **How often do you pray now? Do you make a list? How could a prayer journal help or hurt your prayer life?**

• Listen only to Christian music. **What kind of music is on your mp3 player? What would Jesus say about your selection of music?**

• Pray for an hour each morning. **How often do you think you need to pray each day?**

• Get straight As in school. **How well does God want you to do in school? Is what you are doing in school honoring Jesus?**

When the time drew near for David to die, he gave a charge to Solomon his son. "I am about to go the way of all the earth," he said. "So be strong, act like a man, and observe what the LORD your God requires: Walk in obedience to him, and keep his decrees and commands, his laws and regulations, as written in the Law of Moses. Do this so that you may prosper in all you do and wherever you go." (1 Kings 2:1-3)

3. Use this activity to talk about the benefits of obedience. Ask, "How does obedience protect us?"

4. These true/false statements will help your group members get into a faith discussion about Psalm 72:1-20. This Psalm of David was a prayer that showed David's love for Solomon. David knew that as Israel's new king, Solomon would need divine guidance and intervention if he was to succeed.

5. Use this true-to-life situation to talk together about how a relationship or walk with Jesus is great advice. King David gave his son, Solomon, good advice when he told him to obey God—and it's still good advice today.

THE CLOSE

Everyone is putting advice into practice—including you. Your parents, pastor, friends all give advice to you on how to live your life. But living for the Lord is the best advice you will ever receive. You can say "yes" or "no" to that advice—saying yes is the smartest, best response.

Solomon Gets His Wish

What do you want God to give you?

1. Circle all the words that best describe Solomon before he asked God for wisdom:

Conceited	Arrogant	Unselfish	Modest
Dumb	Vain	Bossy	Humble
Greedy	Reckless	Mean	Egocentric
Sensible	Generous		

For by the grace given me I say to every one of you: Do not think of yourself more highly than you ought, but rather think of yourself with sober judgment, in accordance with the faith God has distributed to each of you. (Romans 12:3)

2. Underline the words in #1 that best describe you.

3. Solomon asked God for wisdom to make right instead of wrong decisions. What decisions do you need wisdom from God to make correctly?

   ❑ I need God to help me make every decision.
   ❑ I need God to help me make most decisions.
   ❑ I need God to help me make some decisions.
   ❑ I don't need God to help me make any decisions.

4. Solomon pleased God by asking for wisdom instead of wealth, a long life, or the destruction of his enemies. Which requests are pleasing to God?

   ❑ Easiest possible classes
   ❑ Wisdom to make good decisions
   ❑ Willingness to take responsibility for myself
   ❑ Enough money to buy whatever I want
   ❑ Positive attitude with my parents
   ❑ Desire to read the Bible
   ❑ Strength to be a better friend

5. Darcy listened to the TV preacher that her grandmother watched every week. Darcy was visiting for the day and sat beside her grandmother while she watched. The preacher was saying that if people would send him money, he would pray for them, and they would get what they wanted. He read some letters from people who asked him to pray for them to be healed—but others asked for things like a bigger house or car. One guy even asked the preacher to pray for a vacation! Most people seemed interested in themselves and "stuff." Darcy knew that her parents got tired when she and her brothers and sister constantly asked them for stuff. *And since God is definitely busier than my parents,* she thought, *do people really think that they should bother God with these kinds of requests?*

   What would you ask for?

READ OUT LOUD

Solomon recognized his limitations. He was probably about 20 years old when he became king and knew he lacked the experience to rule Israel. We find him worshiping God (see 2 Chronicles 1:6-7) the night before the Lord appeared to him in a dream that would change his life forever. God asked him what he wanted the most. Read the story from 1 Kings 35:5-15.

ASK

Who do you ask when you need money?

DISCUSS, BY THE NUMBERS

1. Read Romans 12:3 out loud. Solomon, early in his rule, thought of those he ruled more than he thought of himself. In spite of all the power he had as King over Israel, Solomon was humble.

   Note: As Solomon got older his preoccupation with women pushed him to self-centeredness. Ask, "Why do you think King Solomon, with all his wisdom, allowed women to be his downfall?"

   For by the grace given me I say to every one of you: Do not think of yourself more highly than you ought, but rather think of yourself with sober judgment, in accordance with the faith God has distributed to each of you.
   (Apostle Paul in Romans 12:3)

2. Use this exercise to talk about the benefits of humility over preoccupation with self. Explore each of the words to take a picture of the overall group. Is your group more selfless or selfish? How can your group members think more about others (without thinking less about themselves)?

3. Solomon wanted to lead the Israelites in his kingdom through fairness and justice. He wanted to make the right decisions as he ruled the kingdom his father, King David, had established, so Solomon asked God for wisdom. Use this exercise to talk about the wisdom you and your group members need from God. They don't need God to tell them what color of shoes they should wear, but they need God to give them direction regarding what video games they play or how they talk about others.

4. Ask, "What is the common denominator of the requests that most please God?" The answer: God is most pleased with selfless, others-oriented requests that lead to growth in our relationships with God and others.

5. Use this true-to-life situation to discuss together what you and your group members would ask for. Ask, "How self-centered were our responses? Did we ask for anything that would benefit others?"

THE CLOSE

God gave Solomon a gift—the chance to ask for anything he wanted. And guess what? We have the same opportunity. We can ask God for anything we want. God will grant requests that honor him, and if we ask for wisdom when going through tough times, God will grant you that wisdom (see James 1:5-6). Do you need patience? Just ask God. The Lord is waiting for you to ask for things that will further his kingdom on earth!

Each of the following activities are taken from Bible verses probably written by Solomon.

Solomon Uses His Wisdom to Judge Fairly

Solomon's wisdom can assist us all

1. Which of the four statements best describes you?

❏ I always respect the Lord and never hate wisdom and good advice from adults.

❏ I mostly respect the Lord and hardly ever hate wisdom and good advice from adults.

❏ I sometimes respect the Lord and sometimes hate wisdom and good advice from adults.

❏ I never respect the Lord and always reject wisdom and good advice from adults.

The fear of the LORD is the beginning of knowledge, but fools despise wisdom and instruction. (Proverbs 1:7)

2. Respond to each statement with a Y (yes), N (no), or MS (maybe so).

___ My parents think I make bad friendship decisions.

___ My teachers think I make bad friendship decisions.

___ People at my church think I make bad friendship decisions.

___ My friends think I make bad friendship decisions.

___ I think I make bad friendship decisions.

Do not set foot on the path of the wicked or walk in the way of evildoers. Avoid it, do not travel on it; turn from it and go on your way. (Proverbs 4:14-15)

3. I do what my parents ask of me . . .

❏ . . . all the time.   ❏ . . . sometimes.   ❏ . . . never.

❏ . . . most of the time.   ❏ . . . hardly ever.

My son, keep your father's command and do not forsake your mother's teaching. Bind them always on your heart; fasten them around your neck. When you walk, they will guide you; when you sleep, they will watch over you; when you awake, they will speak to you. (Proverbs 6:20-22)

4. What do you think? Read the statements and respond with A (agree) or D (disagree).

___ A friend's secret is always safe with me.

___ My friends keep secrets I tell them.

___ My friends would say I'm trustworthy.

___ If I'm told something in confidence, I never share it with others.

___ I only gossip about rumors that are true.

A gossip betrays a confidence, but a trustworthy person keeps a secret. (Proverbs 11:13)

READ OUT LOUD

God granted Solomon's wish—the wisdom to rule Israel and know the difference between right and wrong. He was young and knew he needed the wisdom that only God could give if he were to be successful. One day two women came to him, both claiming a baby belonged to each of them. Solomon decided to . . . well, you can read the story from 1 Kings 3:16-28.

ASK

Do you know the difference between right and wrong?

DISCUSS, BY THE NUMBERS

1. Read the verse out loud. Look at the four statements as a group. Decide which statement best describes your group. Usually the group will pick the middle two statements. Discuss why "sometimes" hating wisdom and good advice from adults leads to a lack of respect for God (and vice versa).

2. Each statement examines a friendship choice from a particular perspective. First ask, "Why are parents so concerned about friendship choices?" Usually it's because parents know from their own experiences—or from others' experiences—that friends are a tremendous influence for good or for evil. Talk about each of the other statements (teachers, people at church, friends, self). Ask, "What have you learned about your friendships from looking at these statements?"

3. Create a list on flip-chart paper (big enough for everyone in the group to see) of all the things parents say to kids who are your group members' ages. Then read through the list out loud, checking off statements that are important to follow. Here's a short list of parent statements:
   • Don't talk to strangers.
   • Don't smoke marijuana.
   • Take responsibility for your actions.
   • Do your homework.
   • Remember your manners.
   • Learn another language while you can.
   • Don't watch too much TV.
   • You shouldn't drink until you're 21.
   • You can't have a tattoo.
   • Take your vitamins.
   • Go to bed or you'll be tired tomorrow.
   • Get your chores done.
   • Eat your vegetables.
   • Change your underwear.
   • No, you're not the center of the universe.

4. Most secrets between friends need to be kept. There are some, however, that we need to tell others. For example, if a young person tells a friend that she is using drugs, a trustworthy adult needs to know. This verse talks about being a gossip or someone who spreads rumors. A good rule of thumb: If the secret isn't hurting the friend who told it (or someone else), then keep it; but please tell the secret to a caring adult if keeping the secret hurts the friend who told it (or someone else). Take a minute and identify the kinds of secrets that friends should keep and those that need to be revealed.

THE CLOSE

We looked at five Bible passages from the book of Proverbs—a book mostly written by King Solomon. God gave Solomon wisdom and will give us wisdom, too. While having God's wisdom won't guarantee a trouble-free life, following that wisdom certainly can minimize the mistakes we might otherwise make and sins we might otherwise commit.

1. What do you think? A (agree) or D (disagree)?

___ All gods other than the God of the Bible are false.
___ The worship of other gods leads people to do despicable things.
___ Stuff can become a god.
___ Americans usually worship the wrong god.
___ You can worship more than one god at a time.
___ You can worship other gods and still get to heaven.

> **31. 1 Kings 17:1-24**
>
> # Elijah Speaks the Truth
>
> God says it, and we do it

2. God protected and provided for Elijah while he was in hiding. Baal did nothing for Ahab or Israel to reverse the drought or famine. This should have convinced the followers of Baal to turn to God.

❑ I strongly agree.   ❑ I agree.   ❑ I disagree.   ❑ I strongly disagree.

3. What do you do?

❑ I am like Elijah. I do exactly what God wants me to do.
❑ I am usually like Elijah. I usually, but not always, do what God wants me to do.
❑ I am unlike Elijah. I never do what God wants me to do.

4. Mark these statements T (true) or F (false).

___ I hope God never tests my faith like he did the widow.
___ God has used circumstances to test my faith more than once.
___ I don't like problems that test my faith.
___ I've watched God test others' faith.
___ I want to grow my faith now so that when it's tested I'll do what God wants.

5. "Hey Matt," called Aaron. "Are you going to that dumb Bible club meeting?"

Matt thought for a minute. Should he say "yes" and risk ridicule? Aaron had a reputation for being something of a bully. If Aaron didn't like Matt's answer, it could go badly for Matt. Aaron might beat up Matt or start calling him names at school.

"Yeah," said Matt, saying a quick prayer that God would be with him as he talked to Aaron. Matt hoped God would be on his side as he told the truth. "Why?"

"You're the only person I know who goes to it, and I wanted to check it out," Aaron answered. "I don't want to go alone."

Matt was shocked but not completely; he knew God was with him as he told the truth.

What might have happened if Matt had lied?

READ OUT LOUD

Ahab was the king of Israel. He made the worship of Baal the national religion and constructed a Baal temple and got plenty of Baal priests. Ahab's wife, Jezebel, tried to get rid of the worship of God by persecuting God's prophets. So God called Elijah, a powerful prophet, to counter King Ahab's promotion of Baal. Elijah was quickly introduced at the beginning of today's story. The authority of God behind him, Elijah predicted a drought and famine as punishment for Ahab's idolatry. Read the story from 1 Kings 17:1-24.

ASK

How do you know someone is speaking the truth to you?

DISCUSS, BY THE NUMBERS

1. See commentary in bold after each statement. (Also read out loud Deuteronomy 11:16-17. The Lord had warned Israel not to turn to other gods. He even warned of drought and famine as punishment. King Ahab seemed to have triggered this punishment. God really, really hates idolatry.)

- All gods other than the God of the Bible are false. **God really, really hates idolatry. God created us to be in relationship with him. Christ died to make this a reality. When we worship false gods—money or stuff or anything else—we laugh in the face of our Creator.**

- The worship of other gods leads people to do despicable things. **Sometimes it does. By not acknowledging God and doing what God commands, people are free to do all kinds of evil. Other gods can include power or wealth, so you can be an atheist and still worship other "gods." When you look at past and present dictators around the world, you see them doing all kinds of despicable things.**

- Stuff can become a god. **It is the god of many people in America.**

- Americans usually worship the wrong god. **Unfortunately this is a growing trend; many Americans worship the god of materialism or the god of self or the gods of other religions.**

- You can worship more than one god at a time. **Yes. You can worship power and wealth. You can worship multiple gods as the Hindus or the Mormons do. And you can try to worship God and money at the same time, but as Jesus told us, this is impossible (see Matthew 6:24).**

- You can worship other gods and still get to heaven. **This is false according to the Bible. Jesus is the only way, the only truth, and the only life (see John 14:6).**

Be careful, or you will be enticed to turn away and worship other gods and bow down to them. Then the LORD's anger will burn against you, and he will shut up the heavens so that it will not rain and the ground will yield no produce, and you will soon perish from the good land the LORD is giving you. (Deuteronomy 11:16-17)

2. Ask, "Why do you think the evidence of God's power is often not enough to convince people to turn to Jesus?"

3. Ask, "How many of us would be like Elijah, doing what the Lord asks without question?" Read Mark 12:30 out loud. Discuss what our lives look like when we love God with all our hearts (totally fixated), souls (spirits), minds (intellect), and strength (physical, mental, and emotional stamina).

"Love the Lord your God with all your heart and with all your soul and with all your mind and with all your strength." (Jesus in Mark 12:30)

4. See commentary in bold after each statement:

- I hope God never tests my faith like he did with the widow. **Jesus promises us trouble (see John 16:33).**

- God has used life circumstances to test my faith more than once. **God accepts us as we are— but refuses to leave us there. God wants to strengthen our faith, and that usually comes through trouble, not through good times.**

- I don't like problems that test my faith. **We don't often claim the promise of Jesus (see John 16:33 again).**

- I've watched God test others' faith. **Help your group members identify times of testing in their own lives, as well as in the lives of members of your congregation. This can help your group members better understand positive aspects of life's difficulties.**

- I want to grow my faith now so that when it's tested I'll do what God wants. **Ask, "Isn't it better to learn how to trust in Jesus now rather than wait until the difficult times come?" Remind your group that difficult times are part of all people's lives, whether or not they follow Christ!**

5. Use this true-to-life situation to talk together about obedience. Ask, "How was Matt obedient to God? How was he disobedient?"

THE CLOSE

Elijah showed us how to obey God. God said it, and we're to do it. Elijah made it look easy. But it's not often as easy as Elijah made it look. But the more we practice obedience to God, the easier it becomes. Let's practice every day until we've got it down!

Choose the Lord . . . or Baal

Jesus . . . or the world—we can't have both

1. **In 1 Kings Elijah asked the people of Israel to make a choice: Baal or the one true God. We make many things in our lives "gods"—things that take us away from our relationships with Christ. Which of the following things could become your "god" if you're not careful?**

   ❏ Internet games   ❏ Movies   ❏ Social media
   ❏ Cell phone   ❏ Music   ❏ TV

   Elijah went before the people and said, "How long will you waver between two opinions? If the LORD is God, follow him; but if Baal is God, follow him." But the people said nothing. (1 Kings 18:21)

2. **Diane really wanted to go to her friend Beth's sleepover. Unfortunately it was this Saturday night. Her parents didn't like Diane missing church on Sunday morning, so that meant she probably wouldn't be able to go to Beth's party. *Arghhhhh!* she thought. *Why do friends always have sleepovers on Saturday nights?* Plus now Beth would give her a hard time about having to go to church instead of her party. Diane's friends just didn't understand why she *had* to go to church.**

   What do you think is going on with Diane's relationship with Christ?

3. **Elijah was the only prophet on the mountain with the 450 prophets of Baal. How often do you feel like you're the only person in your circle of friends who's following Christ?**

   ❏ All the time   ❏ Most of the time   ❏ Sometimes   ❏ Hardly ever   ❏ Never

4. **Elijah points out what a small god Baal really is—as opposed to the God of the Bible, who's a bigger God than we can even imagine. So, how do we limit God's size and power?**

   ❏ Behave as though the gods of other religions are real
   ❏ Fear what others might think of us if they catch us praying
   ❏ Don't live like the resurrection of Jesus really happened
   ❏ Define our problems as too big for God
   ❏ Fail to show gratitude for everything God's done for us
   ❏ Haven't read the biblical stories of God's awesome power
   ❏ Lack faith in the big, big God of the Bible

5. **Elijah's people turned their backs on the Lord, and Elijah so wanted them to come back to God. This is why he asked God to answer his prayer that fire would consume the sacrifice and the altar soaked with water. How often do people you know turn their backs on Jesus?**

   ❏ All the time   ❏ Now and then
   ❏ More than you think   ❏ I don't know anyone who's done this.

READ OUT LOUD

No rain had fallen for three years. The Kingdom of Israel was in the third year of a famine. God then commanded Elijah—a prophet we know little about—to go to Ahab, the king of Israel. Elijah proposed a contest between God and Baal. Ahab agrees to the proposal and the two head up Mt. Carmel. Read the incredible account found in 1 Kings 18:16-46.

ASK

What's fun about contests? What's not fun about them?

DISCUSS, BY THE NUMBERS

1. Explore the list and decide when each becomes part of the "worldly system"—i.e., the system of sin/brokenness that Satan rules. For example, "music" becomes part of the worldly system when the listener puts "garbage into her or his mind." Read out loud 1 Kings 18:21 and then explore, "Can you have Jesus *and* the world? Why would you want to have the 'world' if you already have Jesus?" Discuss together how a "fast" from each of the things listed could help your group members stay focused on Jesus.

   > Elijah went before the people and said, "How long will you waver between two opinions? If the LORD is God, follow him; but if Baal is God, follow him." But the people said nothing.
   > (1 Kings 18:21)

2. Answer the question together, "What do you think is going on with Diane's relationship with Christ?" Also ask, "Do you think Diane's friends will help or hinder her future relationship with Christ?" "How could Diane go to Beth's party and grow her relationship with Jesus?" "What could Diane do to share Jesus with her friends?"

3. We may believe we're the only people at our schools and teams who live for Christ, but today's story paints a different picture. Obadiah—an employee of the worldly court of Ahab and Jezebel—chose to be a God-follower. Obadiah hid 100 prophets, protecting them from certain death. Obadiah was silent about his relationship with God while at work because he would have lost his job and probably his life, but he still found a way to serve God. Elijah, on the other hand, was public about his relationship with the God of Israel. Ask, "Who are you most like—Obadiah or Elijah?"

4. Each is an example of how we limit God's size and power. Tell stories from your own life of how you've done this and ask for stories from your group members, too. Discuss together ways in which you and your group members can counter our tendencies to make God smaller.

5. Talk about why it often takes difficult times to get those who've turned away from Christ to come back to him. Pray together for those your group members know who've turned their backs on Jesus.

THE CLOSE

We have a choice every day: We get to choose Jesus or the world. While it's not always easy, we can put Jesus at the center of our lives so that every choice we make considers how our relationship with Christ is affected.

Elijah's Pity Party

Things aren't always as bad as they seem

1. How many people do you know who are like Jezebel, always putting Jesus down?

- ❏ None
- ❏ Not many
- ❏ Some
- ❏ Quite a few
- ❏ Too many

2. After a great spiritual success on Mt. Carmel, Elijah fell apart and fled. What has been a great spiritual success for you?

- ❏ Camp
- ❏ Worship time
- ❏ Personal Bible study
- ❏ Times of service to others
- ❏ Prayer time
- ❏ Fasting
- ❏ Witnessing

3. Circle the words you believe best describe how Elijah felt in today's story.

Abandoned	Happy	Discouraged	Hopeful	Victorious	Confused	Sad
Distressed	Blessed	Overjoyed	Mad	Scared	Bewildered	Lonely

4. Do you agree or disagree with this statement?

God is the same today as in the day of Elijah.
❏ I agree.   ❏ I disagree.   ❏ I'm not sure.

5. Georgia looked at the photos the missionaries were showing. They were updating the projects that money from their church was helping fund. The children in the photos were orphans and would probably have starved to death if they hadn't been taken into the mission school. Some looked too weak to even stand. Then Georgia remembered complaining about the cold cereal she "had" to eat for breakfast and thought, *I really don't have it bad at all.*

Why do you suppose you complain so much?
What does complaining do to your relationship with Christ?
How could you express more gratitude for God's blessings?

6. What do you think—yes or no?

___ Do you wish God would show you his power like he did for Elijah?
___ Do you believe God is interested in you like he was interested in Elijah?
___ Do you think God has a plan for you like he had one for Elijah?

READ OUT LOUD

Jezebel hated God so much that the miraculous, all-consuming fire sent by God to consume the sacrifice didn't faze her. She wouldn't put her faith in God no matter what God did. Instead she wanted Elijah dead. Elijah had experienced a great spiritual success on Mt. Carmel. The prophets of Baal were gone. The rain had fallen. The drought was over. The people had witnessed God's power. But Elijah was running for his life, and things quickly went from good to bad. Read the story out loud in 1 Kings 19:1-18.

ASK

How fast can you run a mile?

DISCUSS, BY THE NUMBERS

1. Discuss together why your group members think the "Jezebels" do what they do. Ask, "What motivates the 'Jezebels' to oppose Jesus?"

2. Ask, "What usually happens after spiritual successes?" Often spiritual lows follow spiritual highs. Perhaps the evil one is on the attack and opposing spiritual successes. Or maybe God is instructing us how to more fully trust in Jesus. Whatever the reason your group members will experience the same thing that happened to Elijah. This exercise is your chance to lead a faith conversation on the question, "Why do you think God lets us go through good times, then bad times, so close together?"

3. Talk together about the words your group members circled. Discuss what should be done when your group members feel like Elijah. Ask, "What did Elijah do right? What did Elijah do that wasn't so right?"

4. Your group members may not think of Christ as existing in the Old Testament. Talk about the dependability of the unchanging triune God. The Lord was there for Elijah in the midst of his crisis of faith, and Jesus will be there for your group members' difficulties.

5. Use this true-to-life situation to discuss together the importance of gratitude—especially when things don't seem to be going our way. Elijah made things worse than they were. Ask, "What might have happened to Elijah's faith and attitude if he would've trusted that God was in charge?" Remember, God told Elijah that 7,000 Israelites had *not* bowed to Baal. This showed that Elijah wasn't alone.

6. See commentary in bold after each question:
   - Do you wish God would show you his power like he did for Elijah? **Talk together about how God shows his power today through working in our lives and in the lives of others.**
   - Do you believe God is interested in you like he was interested in Elijah? **God loves your group members more than you ever could—and more than they realize. God loves them so much that God can't love them in any greater way, and God won't love them any less.**
   - Do you think God has a plan for you like he had a plan for Elijah? **God had a plan for Elijah just as God has a plan for each of your group members. Talk with your group about how God revealed his plan for you.**

THE CLOSE

Elijah experienced a spiritual setback after he left Mt. Carmel. Things went from good to bad to worse. Elijah, feeling sorry for himself, saw no hope for the future; the bad guys were winning. But Elijah failed to see that there were still God-followers and prophets other than himself. He lost sight of the goodness and power of God. That can happen to us, too. Remember, when you feel far away from God . . . guess who moved!

Elisha Wants to Be a Spiritual Leader

What kind of spiritual leader do you want to be?

1. Answer the following three questions with a YES or a NO.

___ Are there students at your school who are spiritual leaders?
___ Are these spiritual leaders having a positive influence?
___ Are you a spiritual leader at your school?

2. Elijah was Elisha's spiritual mentor (someone who gives you spiritual advice, like a tutor). Why might you need a spiritual mentor?

❑ I need someone who can help me grow in my relationship with Jesus.
❑ I need someone to explain the Bible to me.
❑ I need someone who can teach me how to live a life of faith.
❑ I need someone to do my homework for me.
❑ I need someone to teach me how to cut classes without getting caught.
❑ I need someone praying for me every day.
❑ I need someone willing to listen to my problems.

3. What do you think?

	Definitely	Sometimes	Nope
I want to be a spiritual leader.	❑ Definitely	❑ Sometimes	❑ Nope
I'm willing to learn about being a spiritual leader.	❑ Definitely	❑ Sometimes	❑ Nope
I'm afraid to be a spiritual leader.	❑ Definitely	❑ Sometimes	❑ Nope
I can name 10 spiritual leaders in my church.	❑ Definitely	❑ Sometimes	❑ Nope
I already am a spiritual leader.	❑ Definitely	❑ Sometimes	❑ Nope

4. "Don't you go to Eastside Christian Church?" the girl asked Kayla in their school hallway.
   Kayla knew the girl was an eighth-grader but had never really talked to Kayla before. Not many people at her school knew Kayla was a Christian—but Kayla didn't know that this girl went to her church! It made Kayla kind of uncomfortable to talk like this at school. What if one of her friends heard? They'd probably think it was funny.
   "Yes," said Kayla. "Why do you ask?"

   Do you think Kayla should be more open at school about her faith? Why or why not?

5. Elijah was taken to heaven in a chariot of fire. Do you think you will go to heaven?

❑ Not really   ❑ Maybe   ❑ For sure

READ OUT LOUD

Elijah, one of the great prophets of the Old Testament, was about to be taken into heaven. He, along with Elisha, visited the schools of the prophets in the towns of Bethel, Jericho, and near the Jordan River. These visits were probably meant to encourage these prophets—leaders of the God-followers who were left in Israel. Elisha very much wanted to be a spiritual leader, taking up where Elijah would leave off. Read the story found in 2 Kings 2:1-18.

ASK

Who is a leader you would follow?

DISCUSS, BY THE NUMBERS

1. Use this activity to start a faith conversation about the desired qualities in a spiritual leader. Ask each of your group members to name those who've had the most faith influence on them.
2. Discuss together how a spiritual mentor—someone we trust and look up to—could help us grow in our relationships with Jesus Christ.
3. See commentary in bold after each statement:
   - I want to be a spiritual leader. **Explore why it's important to become more like Jesus Christ so that you can be an example to others.**
   - I'm willing to learn about being a spiritual leader. **This will launch you on an exciting journey of following Christ. Remember: Christ makes life exciting!**
   - I'm afraid to be a spiritual leader. **Fear is natural and one of the tools Satan uses to frustrate us and keep us from becoming all that God wants us to be.**
   - I can name 10 spiritual leaders in the congregation. **Use this statement as an opportunity to look at those in your congregation who, though flawed, are examples of spiritual leadership.**
   - I already am a spiritual leader. **Talk together about ways your group members are already examples to others of what it means to live for Jesus.**

4. Growth of any kind requires that we move out of our comfort zones. This is risky because we like to be comfortable. (That's why it's called a "comfort zone" to begin with.) Kayla needed to get out of her comfort zone. It would be okay for her to feel uncomfortable as she talked about her faith. Explore with your group what new opportunities they could try that would get them out of their faith comfort zones.
5. A common question asked by Billy Graham and other evangelists a generation ago was, "If you died tonight, would you know for certain that you were going to heaven?" Those today in the first third of life don't often ponder this question. Ask, "Why do you suppose people today in the United States and Canada don't often ask this question to themselves or others?"

THE CLOSE

Too often today we require very little from ourselves or young people, whether in or out of our churches. Expectations set low are always matched by low results. But there is power in expecting more from ourselves and others. Jesus set high expectations for the disciples, and look what they accomplished with the power of the Holy Spirit. Set high spiritual expectations for your young people. Expect that they can be spiritual leaders. Give them meaningful leadership roles. They can and will meet those expectations.

An Unusual Healing

God's ways are not always our ways

1. **God uses all kinds of people who don't necessarily follow Jesus to correct me.**

   ❑ I agree.
   ❑ I disagree.
   ❑ I'm not sure.
   ❑ I hope not.

2. **God used leprosy to keep Naaman humble. How humble are you?**

   ❑ I need to be more humble.
   ❑ I'm humble enough.
   ❑ I'm too humble.

3. **The Syrians invaded Israel. An Israelite girl was taken captive as a slave. She worked for the family of a Syrian military leader.**

   Was this situation fair to the girl?
   Was this situation fair to the girl's parents, now separated from her?
   Why do you suppose this girl, forced into slavery, told her owner about God's prophet?

4. **Naaman thought he deserved better treatment from Elisha and God. Have you ever thought God treated you unfairly?**

   ❑ Often
   ❑ Sometimes
   ❑ Never

5. **Carlos didn't understand his grandma at all. She was always praying about something, usually her family. She would ask God for specific things: jobs, healing, or peace for anyone who was hurting. Sometimes her prayers were answered the way she hoped; sometimes not. It didn't seem to matter to Carlos' grandma. She once told him that God always answered prayers—sometimes we just didn't understand the answer. "Keep praying Carlos," she said. "God knows what he's doing."**

   Why do you think Carlos didn't understand his grandma?

6. **I sometimes treat God like a genie.**

   ❑ True
   ❑ False

READ OUT LOUD

God's people were under attack from Syria. The Israelites' worship of other gods had gone on long enough, and God used the Syrian army to punish them. The head of the Syrian army, a man named Naaman, had contracted leprosy. Like anyone experiencing an incurable disease, Naaman wished for a miraculous cure. Naaman learned something about the God of the Bible—that God's ways are not always what people expect. Read the story found in 2 Kings 5:1-16.

ASK

Do you think God cures people today of incurable diseases?

DISCUSS, BY THE NUMBERS

1. Ask, "Does God correct us when we sin?" The Bible teaches that God will punish those who choose to make themselves the center of the universe (unbelievers) but disciplines those who believe. See Hebrews 12:7 below.

> Endure hardship as discipline;
> God is treating you as his children.
> For what children are not disciplined
> by their father? (Hebrews 12:7)

Ask, "How does discipline when we sin help us get closer to Jesus?"

2. Look at a few verses from Psalms to see what God thinks of humility:

> You save the humble but bring low those
> whose eyes are haughty. (Psalm 18:27)

> He guides the humble in what is right and
> teaches them his way. (Psalm 25:9)

> For the LORD takes delight in his people; he
> crowns the humble with victory. (Psalm 149:4)

3. The nation of Israel was being punished by God for their idolatry. Even though the nation had abandoned God, there still were some who loved the Lord. The girl in the story was one of those God-followers. Most likely she grew up in a home where God was honored. See commentary in bold after each question:

- Was this situation fair to the girl? **It wasn't fair from a human perspective. Sin causes evil, and this young girl was a victim of the sinfulness of both Israel and Syria.**
- Was this situation fair to the girl's parents, now separated from her? **It was unfair, but fortunately they raised her to be a God-follower and love her enemies.**
- Why do you think this girl, forced into slavery, told her owner about God's prophet? **She loved the Lord in spite of her situation and thus loved her enemies. This love paid off in that Naaman and his household heard about the one true God.**

4. Don't discount the stories your group members share about their anger, disappointment, and other feelings about God. Do let your group members share. Then tell your God story. Often we feel entitled because others have treated us badly. We then, because of a distorted theology of God, blame God for our situations.

5. Use this true-to-life situation to talk about praying in line with God's will. We often pray our list of entitlements then blame God when God doesn't come through for us. Carlos had not yet learned what his grandmother already knew—God's ways are not our ways. Thank God for knowing more than we know and wanting the best for us.

6. Use this question to further cement the truth that God's ways are not our ways. God is not a genie in a bottle ready to pop out and honor our wishes. God is the God of the universe who loves us and wants the best for us even when we pray for something that's not the best.

THE CLOSE

"For my thoughts are not your thoughts, neither are your ways my ways," declares the LORD (God in Isaiah 55:8). Naaman learned this through his grumbling. He came to know a God who expects obedience even when we're not sure what's happening. We too can find deeper relationships with a God who's much bigger than we can possibly imagine. We serve a big God who we can never completely comprehend. Isn't it great?

Elisha Predicts a Miracle Victory

God is working in our lives whether we know it or not

1. Lepers were separated from society because this incurable disease at the time terrified people. What in life terrifies you?

- ❏ School shootings
- ❏ Popular crowd
- ❏ Someone at school might ask me if I believe in Jesus
- ❏ Getting bad grades
- ❏ Losing friends
- ❏ Finding friends
- ❏ Looking different
- ❏ War
- ❏ People finding out who I really am
- ❏ Family finances

2. God wants to do great things in your life like God did by making the Syrians run for their lives.

❏ Not in my life   ❏ Maybe in my life   ❏ Definitely in my life

3. God blessed the four lepers with food and Syrian treasure. God has blessed me with—

- ❏ An awesome family
- ❏ A home
- ❏ Daily food
- ❏ Great Christian friends
- ❏ A good church
- ❏ Health
- ❏ Other: _____

4. For as long as he could remember Bobby had heard his father talk about how his mother had been healed from cancer. Doctors told his father that her tumor was inoperable and that she only had a few months to live. The family would not accept the diagnosis. Bobby's grandfather called their pastor and soon everyone in the church knew and was praying. When his grandmother went in for a checkup three weeks later, the doctor could find no sign of the tumor—as if it were never there. How could people not believe in miracles?

   What kind of miracle do you think it's okay to ask God for? Healing? Money? A friend believing in Jesus?

5. Elisha, God's prophet, was confident in God's word. He believed. The king's officers couldn't believe what God could do. What do you think you would have believed?

- ❏ I would have believed what Elisha said.
- ❏ I would have been confused by what Elisha said.
- ❏ I might have believed what Elisha said.
- ❏ I would have refused to believe what Elisha said.

READ OUT LOUD

God's people living in Samaria were starving to death. The Syrian army had attacked the city, forcing the people behind the safety of their walls. Without much food left, Elisha—God's spokesperson—predicted that an abundance of food was coming. One of the king's officials refused to believe the word of the Lord delivered by Elisha. Read the story from 2 Kings 7:1-20.

ASK

What's the hungriest you've ever been?

DISCUSS, BY THE NUMBERS

1. Use this exercise to begin a faith conversation about how followers of Jesus must be counter-to-the-culture Christians. While everything on the list can lead to fear, followers of Jesus have prayer to guide them. We need not be afraid because the one to whom we pray has the power to overcome the fear that results from each of these listed circumstances.

2. The New Testament, like the Old, speaks of God's desire to do great things in our everyday lives. Often middle school students see God as some higher power intimately involved in the lives of grownups but not their lives. Explore with your group the roadblocks to believing and acting upon this truth.

3. Choose the top-two blessings identified most by your group. Make a master list of all the blessings God has provided them. Use this opportunity to discuss together the importance of great Christian friends who can be a positive influence and your congregation's support of young people.

4. Use this true-to-life situation to discuss the kind of miracles for which we should pray. Middle school students often view God as their own personal genie who, when they need him, pops out of the bottle and must grant them three wishes. Our God is much bigger than a genie. Our God wants us to pray God's will for our lives and the lives of others. Our God waits to hear from us about what we long for, and then he does what's best for us and others.

Our God wants our persistent prayers to align with his will.

5. Decide together what a life would look like if it looked like Elisha's and then what one would look like if it were like the king's officer. The details written about the king's officer were included so that readers could see that Elisha's prediction came true—that God's prophet and God's word could be counted on. God is always faithful.

THE CLOSE

Our God is in the miracle business. God was working on behalf of Israel while they thought they were starving to death. The king's officer had no faith in God. He simply couldn't see God working a miracle to save him and God's people. His lack of faith brought a disastrous result. The idolatry of the Syrian army brought them a disastrous result. God's people living in the city were humbled by their circumstances. God used those circumstances to show their brokenness and need to depend only on him. The God of Israel worked on their behalf. God is our God working in our lives whether we can see his work or not.

1. **What do you think? Y (yes) or N (no)**

____ I pray only when I'm in trouble.
____ I don't think God answers the prayers of youths.
____ I don't have anything important to say to God, so I don't pray too much.
____ I'm not sure why God wants me to pray.
____ I don't see the need for prayer when things are going well in my life.

Nehemiah Shoots an Arrow Prayer

We can pray wherever we are

2. **Respond to each of the following statements with a T (true) or F (false).**

____ I pray more for myself than others.
____ I know that people are praying for me.
____ I pray for others the most when I'm at church.
____ I don't know what to pray for when I pray for others.
____ I pray for Christians around the world.

3. **For which of the following do you need to shoot up an "arrow prayer" like Nehemiah did before he told the king what he wanted him to do.**

❑ When you have a pop quiz
❑ When you're caught lying
❑ When you get home late
❑ When your parents are fighting

❑ When you forgot to do your homework
❑ When you're worried about your family
❑ When you get in an argument with a friend

4. **What do you think? A=Agree D=Disagree DK=Don't Know**

____ Prayer works best in the morning.
____ You can pray anywhere but in government buildings.
____ You can pray for dead people.
____ The best prayer posture is on your knees.
____ You don't have to pray before meals.

5. **Trisha's stepdad usually laughed when he saw her pray before meals. He not only didn't believe in God, but also he didn't want people around him acting as though they believed, either. He thought praying was for weak people. He was really different from her birth-dad. Before Trisha's birth-dad died, he would pray with Trisha. In fact, he was the one who taught Trisha how to pray. He encouraged her to pray whenever she wanted to talk to God. Trisha decided that she would not stop praying before meals or any other time she wanted to pray. She would just pray silently so that her stepdad would never know. She hoped that this was okay with God.**

What do you wish you could say to Trisha? To Trisha's stepdad? To Trisha's mom?

READ OUT LOUD

Nehemiah lived in a foreign land. He served as the food and drink tester for King Artaxerxes, meaning that if food or drink meant for the king was poisoned, Nehemiah was dead. He wrestled with the Lord in prayer about the condition of his homeland, Israel. He heard that Jerusalem, the capital city, lay in ruins. He wished to go home and help rebuild his nation. Read the story found in Nehemiah 2:1-7.

ASK

What needs to be rebuilt at your house?

DISCUSS, BY THE NUMBERS

1. See commentary in bold after each statement:
   • I pray only when I'm in trouble. **Unfortunately we often treat God like a cash machine—he's there when we need something from him. Ask, "How can we develop a prayer life that isn't based on crisis prayer?"**
   • I don't think God answers the prayers of youths. **Ask, "Where does this kind of thinking come from?" Often young people feel discounted by their congregation, and this can translate into their relationships with God.**
   • I don't have anything important to say to God, so I don't pray too much. **This is a distorted view of self and God that doesn't see the joy in a friendship with Christ.**
   • I'm not sure why God wants me to pray. **If this is an issue for your group, talk together about how your members can learn more about the necessity of prayer.**
   • I don't see the need for prayer when things are going well in my life. **The point is to grow our relationships with Christ in the good times so that we'll be strong in our faith when the bad times come—because they will come.**
2. Nehemiah, though he was scared, could boldly approach King Artaxerxes because he had already spent time with God regarding the issue. Far too many of our prayers are about us and our needs and wants. This activity can help your group members examine how much time they spend in prayer

for others versus the time they spend in prayer for themselves.
3. An "arrow prayer" is quickly sent to God in the midst of a busy day. No matter what we're doing, we can shoot up an arrow prayer to God for strength, for a friend in need, for a teacher, or for any immediate issue requiring divine guidance.
4. See commentary in bold after each statement:
   • Prayer works best in the morning. **We can pray at any time.**
   • You can pray anywhere but in government buildings. **We can pray anywhere. Nehemiah prayed before he spoke to a king.**
   • You can pray for dead people. **Nehemiah mentioned the graves of his ancestors probably because King Artaxerxes would have viewed disturbing the dead as sacrilegious and more likely would want to help Nehemiah. But this doesn't mean we pray for the dead. Their time has come and gone.**
   • The best prayer posture is on your knees. **There is no best posture. It can be helpful, however, to pray in different body positions to show reverence to God and to help keep us focused.**
   • You don't have to pray before meals. **We aren't required to pray before meals. When we do, the purpose is to show gratitude to God.**
5. Use this true-to-life situation to discuss difficult situations your group members face regarding their prayer lives.

THE CLOSE

We can pray at any time, in any situation we find ourselves. Nehemiah prayed at length when he heard what happened in Jerusalem. He was prepared to speak to King Artaxerxes because he had prayed ahead of time. Even still Nehemiah prayed before he presented his request to the king. This is a good reminder for us to pray again and again for ourselves and others, no matter what we find ourselves doing.

1. **At school (or other activities like my sports teams) I get made fun of for being a Christian—**

   ❏ Often
   ❏ Sometimes
   ❏ Rarely
   ❏ Never

2. **In addition to leading God's people in rebuilding the wall, Nehemiah prayed. How often during a typical day should a Jesus-follower pray?**

   ❏ No more than once
   ❏ Once, if necessary
   ❏ Only when necessary—like before a test or quiz
   ❏ A couple of times
   ❏ All the time throughout the day and night

3. **Revenge hurts me as much as the object of my revenge.**

   ❏ Strongly agree
   ❏ Agree
   ❏ Don't know
   ❏ Disagree
   ❏ Strongly disagree

4. **Nehemiah and God's people prayed as some of them kept rebuilding the wall around Jerusalem while others stood guard. What do you think is the balance between prayer and action? (Choose one.)**

   ❏ Why pray? What's the use?
   ❏ Don't sit around praying, just get the job done.
   ❏ Pray and sit back and wait to see what happens.
   ❏ Pray as though 100 percent of the results depend on God; act as though 100 percent of the results depend on your actions.

5. **Bethany watched her father put the check into the envelope. Every month her family saved spare change and recycled their aluminum cans to raise money to support a child in an African country. They also committed to doing without one luxury each month (e.g., sodas, movies, candy) to help save money to give to their sponsored child. After her father put the check in the envelope he turned to Bethany and said, "Would you pray that the Lord will use this money to help Andreas?"**

   Why do you think Bethany needed to pray?

READ OUT LOUD

God's people, the Jews, were disciplined by God for their idolatry. They were conquered and led away to a foreign land. Years later Nehemiah led a group of Jews from Persia (today's Iran) back to Jerusalem. The enemies of the Jews wanted to prevent them from rebuilding the walls of Jerusalem. Hating the Jews, they didn't want them safe in Jerusalem. Read the story found in Nehemiah 4:1-23.

ASK

Who cares about your safety?

DISCUSS, BY THE NUMBERS

1. While those living in the United States and Canada don't experience the persecution that Christians in other countries face, there is ridicule and teasing for being a Jesus-follower. When Christians live like Jesus, they will be made fun of. Discuss together the ways Christians experience ridicule. Here are some examples:
   • People look at me funny when I pray before lunch at school.
   • People make fun of me for carrying my Bible in my backpack.
   • People apologize when they curse in front of me.
   • People make fun of me for going to Bible study.
2. Analyze how often your group members pray as well as the content of their prayers. Discuss together why your group members believe they pray so much about themselves and less about others. Discuss what your group members think that 1 Thessalonians 5:17 means (see below).

   Rejoice always, pray continually, give thanks in all circumstances; for this is God's will for you in Christ Jesus. (1 Thessalonians 5:16-18)

3. It may seem as though Nehemiah hated his neighbor, but actually the style of writing is similar to the Psalms in which the writer calls upon God to take revenge rather than the writer taking revenge. Use this opportunity to look at prayer as conversing with God about our feelings—even the desire to take revenge upon others. Read Romans 12:19 out loud to your group.

   Do not take revenge, my dear friends, but leave room for God's wrath, for it is written: "It is mine to avenge; I will repay," says the Lord. (Romans 12:19)

4. Nehemiah knew God could be depended upon for protection and care. Nehemiah also knew that God gave him a brain to think of ways he could protect and care for himself and God's people. God gave us the smarts, the will, and the power to act for our self-preservation. God's strength, guidance, and power are available to us to do everything we possibly can to bring God's kingdom into reality here on earth. God wants us to pray like 100 percent of the results depend upon God and act as though 100 percent of the results depend upon our actions. Always remember that God has your back as you work to do God's will.
5. Use this true-to-life situation to explore other situations that illustrate what Nehemiah knew and practiced—that we must pray *and* act.

THE CLOSE

God expects us to work, and God expects us to pray. A great leader sees the need for both. Great leaders help people depend upon God for the results God wants while working to achieve those results under the leadership of God's Spirit. Can you pray while you work for God's kingdom?

Ezra Reads the Law Out Loud

How should we respond to God's Word when it's recited aloud?

1. The people of God stood when Ezra opened the Bible because—

(Check statements you believe are true.)
- ❑ they were getting tired of sitting.
- ❑ they wanted to show respect for God's Word.
- ❑ they were ready to go home.
- ❑ they wanted to appear holy to their friends sitting next to them.
- ❑ they wanted to see the PowerPoint slides.
- ❑ standing helped them pay attention to what was read.

2. Do you strongly agree, agree, disagree, or strongly disagree with each of the following statements?

	STRONGLY AGREE	AGREE	DISAGREE	STRONGLY DISAGREE
My parents make me read the Bible.	❑	❑	❑	❑
I like reading the Bible by myself.	❑	❑	❑	❑
I have a plan for reading the Bible.	❑	❑	❑	❑
The Bible is boring.	❑	❑	❑	❑
Reading the Bible can help me know God better.	❑	❑	❑	❑
Reading the Bible won't make me a better person.	❑	❑	❑	❑
I don't understand the Bible when I read it by myself.	❑	❑	❑	❑
I'll get into heaven because I read the Bible.	❑	❑	❑	❑

3. God's people carefully listened to God's Word as it was read out loud. After the reading, the meaning of what was read was explained to them. How is the Bible explained to you in your congregation? Through . . .

- ❑ preaching ❑ drama ❑ music ❑ dance ❑ small groups ❑ prayer
- ❑ other: _____

4. Circle the ends of the sentences that apply to you.

When my congregation sings—
a. I always sing along.
b. I usually sing along.
c. I hardly ever sing along.
d. I never sing along.

When the Bible is read to my congregation—
a. I always pay attention.
b. I usually pay attention.
c. I now and then pay attention.
d. I never pay attention.

When the sermon is preached to my congregation—
a. I always learn something.
b. I often learn something.
c. I sometimes learn something.
d. I never seem to follow along.

READ OUT LOUD

Ezra, a Bible teacher in Old Testament times, was probably the first person to return to Israel from captivity in the Mede-Persian Empire. Then Nehemiah came home to help rebuild. In today's story the Bible of that time was read out loud to the people. It was a long reading and explanation, lasting from early morning until midday. Imagine reading and preaching to your congregation on Sunday for six hours! Find the story in Nehemiah 8:1-12.

ASK

What was the longest church service you've ever attended?

DISCUSS, BY THE NUMBERS

1. Use this activity to encourage your group members to read the Bible more. Don't use this time to beat them up for not reading the Bible; instead build on what your group members are already doing with Bible reading and Bible study.

2. When Ezra opened the Bible, everyone stood to show their respect for and desire to focus on what God had to say. Use this activity to explore together how you and your group members respond when the Bible is read in church or in youth group settings. Ask, "Why is it so easy to get distracted when listening to the Bible being read?"

3. See how many mediums through which the Bible is explained—e.g., preaching, small groups, drama productions, dance, music, skits, videos, Power-Point slides—that your group can name.

4. Singing, Bible reading, and preaching are three ways your congregation worships God. Use this activity to explore how your group members could involve themselves more enthusiastically in these three worship activities. Also explore "why" your congregation does what it does.

> *Ezra praised the LORD, the great God; and all the people lifted their hands and responded, "Amen! Amen!" Then they bowed down and worshiped the LORD with their faces to the ground. (Nehemiah 8:6)*

THE CLOSE

In the United States and Canada there are multiple translations of the Bible in most Christian homes. It's easy and inexpensive to purchase a Bible. Most congregations will even give you one for free if you ask. We are drowning in Bibles! Yet we don't often read them regularly. Wow! What a response to the free availability of the Scriptures! What might happen if we took God's Word more seriously? What might happen if we read the Bible every day? What might happen if we committed to participate in a weekly Bible study? Perhaps we would truly love God with everything in us, as well as love our neighbors as ourselves—which would include our enemies. What do you think?

Mordecai Remained Faithful

Beware of those who want to lead you away from Christ

1. Mordecai openly revealed that he was a God-follower who worshiped the God of the Bible. How open are you with your faith? (Check all of the answers that apply to you.)

   ❏ Open with my family
   ❏ Open with my Christ-follower friends
   ❏ Open with my non-Christian friends
   ❏ Open with my neighbors
   ❏ Open with my teachers
   ❏ Open with my coaches
   ❏ Open with my acquaintances

2. Who are your friends most like?

   ❏ My friends are most like Mordecai. They are willing to say NO to things that aren't good for them.
   ❏ My friends are most like Haman. They try to influence others to do what's wrong.
   ❏ My friends are most like the officials who bowed down to Haman. They usually do whatever is safest or most popular.

3. Haman wanted all the Jews killed because one Jew, Mordecai, refused to worship him—and no Jews would have meant no Jesus, either. Could the evil one, Satan, have been working in the background to destroy God's plan of salvation?

   ❏ Satan doesn't exist.   ❏ It could have been Satan.   ❏ It most definitely was Satan.

4. Mordecai refused to let Haman's "worship me" lead him away from God and his faith. Who or what could lead you away from Christ?

   ❏ Being made fun of
   ❏ Parents divorcing
   ❏ Friend moving away
   ❏ Mormon, Muslim, or Hindu friend
   ❏ Pastor leaving the church
   ❏ Being chosen for a special sports team or drama production
   ❏ Other: _____

5. Little brothers aren't supposed to die. That's just the way it is. Didn't God know this? Didn't God hear their prayers? Didn't God hear Donnie's mom crying at night when she didn't think anyone was listening? Donnie had prayed hard, too. He got down on his knees and asked God to make his brother better. He got down on his knees! Who did that these days? Donnie told God he'd do anything God wanted for the rest of his life. It didn't feel like God was listening. Why wasn't he listening? Plus, Donnie's neighbor Mrs. French said that praying really didn't make any difference; if it was your time to die, you just died.

   What would you say to Donnie?

READ OUT LOUD

The Persian Empire ruled with an iron fist until they were conquered by the Greeks in 331 B.C. The Persians had conquered the Babylonians and kept God's people, the Jews, in captivity away from their homeland, Israel. One of the leaders under King Xerxes was a man named Haman. By order of Xerxes, all officials under Haman were to worship him. Mordecai, one of those officials, refused. Mordecai was clear about his convictions. He knew the Ten Commandments—he was to worship God only. He remained faithful to the God of the Bible even though it could have cost him his life. Read the story found in Esther 3:1-15.

ASK

How clear are the rules at home?

DISCUSS, BY THE NUMBERS

1. It isn't always easy to unapologetically confess our faith as it was for Mordecai. Ask, "Who is easiest to be open with about your faith in Christ?" "Who is most difficult?" Discuss the reasons why for each of the questions. Ask, "Do we always have to be open about our faith with everyone? Why or why not?"

2. This activity gives you the opportunity to discuss the kinds of friends your group members choose. There are three basic choices: 1) friends who can say NO to bad choices; 2) friends who influence others to choose what's wrong; and 3) friends easily swayed by peer pressure.

3. The Bible teaches us that we aren't wrestling with other human beings but against the demonic world. Read Ephesians 6:12 out loud (found below). Use today's story and this verse to talk about the struggle against evil and Satan that we face. Neither God nor Satan is mentioned in the account of Mordecai and Esther, yet this struggle against spiritual forces of darkness is clearly evident. Ask, "How do you think God and Satan were working in the background?" "How does this apply to today?"

> *For our struggle is not against flesh and blood, but against the rulers, against the authorities, against the powers of this dark world and against the spiritual forces of evil in the heavenly realms. (Ephesians 6:12)*

4. We must remain vigilant against anything that can lead us away from Christ. We must also work toward creating a supportive faith community that keeps us close to Jesus. These two things are often in tension and must be balanced. We can't spend all of our time in a vigilant mode without a supportive faith community surrounding us; we also may get too comfortable if we focus all our attention on our faith community without protecting ourselves from everyday distractions.

5. Discuss what Donnie needs to watch out for in this true-to-life situation. Look at similar situations your group members face and identify what they need to watch out for.

THE CLOSE

Some people will intentionally attempt to lead you away from Christ—through temptations, arguments about the existence of God, or simply making fun of you. Mordecai remained faithful because he was a part of a faith community of God-followers (the Jewish people). We are part of a faith community called *the church*. When we stick together as the church, we can encourage one another in our faith. When we wander away, we can easily be led away from Christ. Let's commit to stick together!

1. Esther reached out to her uncle, Mordecai, when he was depressed. Who usually reaches out to you when you're down?

- ❏ Family members
- ❏ Close friends
- ❏ Church members
- ❏ Pastor
- ❏ I keep my problems to myself.
- ❏ Coach
- ❏ Nobody

41. Esther 4:1-17

For Such a Time as This

God places us in situations so we can do good

2. **Do you agree with this statement?**

Like Haman, many people are motivated by greed and arrogance—
❏ I agree.   ❏ I disagree.

3. **Like Esther, I do the right thing for God—**

- ❏ all the time.
- ❏ most of the time.
- ❏ sometimes.
- ❏ hardly ever.

4. **God placed you in the situation you're in today to—**

(Choose one.)
- ❏ tell a specific person about Jesus.
- ❏ encourage someone with no friends.
- ❏ raise money for a cause.
- ❏ serve the church.
- ❏ learn a biblical truth.
- ❏ teach me patience.
- ❏ practice loving my neighbor.

5. **The lunchroom monitor looked so sad. Most kids just pushed past her like she wasn't even there. Some kids would say rude things to her. She never dressed very nicely, and if someone said the wrong thing, she would burst into tears. But she was really nice if you just took the time to talk to her. So Lucy tried to talk to her at least once a day, even if it was only to say hello. Lucy didn't care what the other kids thought. It was the right thing to do.**

How realistic is this situation?

READ OUT LOUD

Mordecai was grief-stricken when he learned about the upcoming destruction of the God-following Jews. So Mordecai sent a messenger to his niece, Queen Esther, asking her to go to her husband King Xerxes and ask him to intervene for her people, God's people, the Jews. Mordecai told his niece that she was in the right place at the right time to do the right thing. Read the story found in Esther 4:1-17.

ASK

Where is the right place to shop for clothes?

DISCUSS, BY THE NUMBERS

1. God often places specific people in our lives so that we can help them or so that they can help us. Share a story of an individual God placed in your life to help you. Ask your group members to share who God uses in their lives to reach out to them. Discuss how they might have been placed in their friends' lives to reach out and help them, too. Ask, "How would God want you to help?"

2. Doing what's right in God's eyes doesn't always motivate us, just as it didn't motivate Haman. Explore what we must do to make God's opinion a priority in our lives. To do this—

   First ask, "What is God's opinion regarding (insert topic or issue here)?"

   Second ask, "Do I care about God's opinion?"

   Mordecai knew God had an opinion regarding the worship of others (see Exodus 20:4). He cared about that opinion and decided to say no to Haman's demand that Mordecai bow down to him in worship.

3. Sometimes we are influencers (like Mordecai) while at other times we are influenced (like Esther). Discuss what it takes to influence others in a positive direction—e.g., courage, conviction, faith. Then discuss how we sometimes need to be persuaded to do the right thing. Ask, "When do you need to be convinced to do what's right?"

4. Read Esther 4:14 out loud. While the book of Esther never mentions the name of God, the author clearly wanted us to see God working in the background to save the Jews. God worked out events so that Esther, a Jew, would become Queen. God positioned her to save the God-following people of Israel so that they could return to their homeland. Use this background information to explore why God has placed you and your group members in their various situations.

   "For if you remain silent at this time, relief and deliverance for the Jews will arise from another place, but you and your father's family will perish. And who knows but that you have come to your royal position for such a time as this?"
   (Esther 4:14)

5. This true-to-life situation can be used as a springboard to discuss similar situations your group members have faced.

THE CLOSE

God placed Esther in her position as Queen. She may have seen her position as something she achieved through her good looks, personality, talent, or brains. While God can use these attributes for good, God also sets up the conditions for us to serve him where we are placed—and we can choose to honor God and do his work or allow God to choose someone else. You have been placed where you are "for such a time as this." What will you choose to do?

Better Than Everyone Else?

Self-importance can backfire

1. Haman's bragging made him feel more important than he actually was. This could happen to me if I'm not careful.

   ❏ Definitely   ❏ Maybe
   ❏ Probably   ❏ Hope not

2. Haman's anger got so out of control that he wanted all the Jews killed. What do you think? Check the box after each statement that best describes you.

	ALWAYS	MOSTLY	SOMETIMES	NEVER
• I let my anger get me into trouble.	❏	❏	❏	❏
• I can choose NOT to let my anger get the best of me.	❏	❏	❏	❏
• I shouldn't be angry because I'm a Christian.	❏	❏	❏	❏
• I get angry at the littlest things.	❏	❏	❏	❏
• My anger turns to rage.	❏	❏	❏	❏

3. Haman's wife and his friends encouraged him to murder Mordecai. Would your parents say that your friends encourage you to make—

   ❏ mostly the right decisions.
   ❏ mostly the wrong decisions.
   ❏ some right and some wrong decisions.

4. What do you think?

   Selfishness leads to a happier life.

   ❏ Always   ❏ Mostly   ❏ Mostly not   ❏ Never

5. Katy was on top of the world. She made it to the final round of her school's spelling contest. If she won, she would advance to the district level. The only problem was that she would have to beat her friend Michelle to do it
   "You can do it," their friend Polly told Katy as they walked into the music room.
   "I know I can beat her," said Katy confidently. "She's just been lucky so far."
   "Uh, Katy," said Polly as she pointed behind Katy. There was Michelle a few feet away; from the look on her face it was obvious she'd heard Katy's comment.

   How do you think Katy should handle this situation? Will her success make her arrogant? Why or why not?

READ OUT LOUD

Haman wanted revenge on Mordecai for not bowing down and worshiping him. Haman's hatred of Mordecai turned to rage when Haman plotted to kill, not just Mordecai—the God-following Jew—but all Jews. Haman wanted to get even with Mordecai in a despicable way. Queen Esther, also a God-following Jew, decided that God had put her into King Xerxes' palace to save her people. Read the story found in Esther 5:1-14.

ASK

When do you most want to "get even" with someone?

DISCUSS, BY THE NUMBERS

1. Discuss situations in which you and your group members find yourselves feeling more important than you really are. Ask, "How could this kind of thinking hurt you or others?"
2. See commentary in bold after each statement:
   - I let my anger get me into trouble. **Explore how our anger gets us into trouble since we don't usually set out to get ourselves into trouble.**
   - I can choose NOT to let my anger get the best of me. **Anger is an emotion—neither good nor bad. It's how we choose to express our anger that gets the best of us.**
   - I shouldn't be angry because I'm a Christian. **Not true. Jesus expressed anger. Again, it's what we do with anger that counts.**
   - I get angry at the littlest things. **A short fuse puts you on a path of hurting yourself and others. Look at what it did to Haman.**
   - My anger turns to rage. **This is a signal that we're not handling our anger appropriately.**
3. Explore the power that friendships have in our lives. Our friends (with both adults and youth) have the power to shape who we become. If we surround ourselves with people who are positive influences, our lives will head in positive directions. The reverse is also true: If we find ourselves drawn to negative influencers, our lives are more likely to head down negative paths. Negative-influence friends can inflate our egos in unhealthy ways, so we should steer clear of them.
4. Explore with your group the pros and cons of selfishness. Then weigh your two lists to see which side "wins"—selfishness or selflessness. The reality is that we fluctuate between the two, so talk about how we can move closer to selflessness through our decisions.
5. Use this true-to-life situation to explore similar situations that you and your group members see happening around them. Talk about how we can learn from the "arrogance" mistakes of others.

THE CLOSE

Too often we think too much of ourselves. Haman certainly did, and it led to his death. While our arrogance won't likely lead to the consequence Haman experienced, we will find that our selfishness can backfire. Our arrogance can backfire by hurting our relationships with others and with God. Our self-importance can get in the way of our achievements. Our cockiness can lead to sin because we begin to believe we deserve more than we're getting. Let's commit to living our lives humbly before the Lord, recognizing all God has blessed us with.

For by the grace given me I say to every one of you: Do not think of yourself more highly than you ought, but rather think of yourself with sober judgment, in accordance with the faith God has distributed to each of you. (Romans 12:3)

A Famous Test

We may never understand God's reasons for our trials

1. **Job really loved God. While Jesus is the one who saves us, we can show evidence of that salvation through our actions. How do you show that you love Jesus?**

   - ❏ Carry a 10-pound Bible to school
   - ❏ Do the best I possibly can with my homework
   - ❏ Wear T-shirts with Christian slogans
   - ❏ Treat my teachers with respect
   - ❏ Pray out loud in the cafeteria during lunch
   - ❏ Recycle
   - ❏ Befriend the unlovely
   - ❏ Display a Christian bumper sticker on the family car
   - ❏ Never talk to non-Christian people my age
   - ❏ Avoid spreading rumors

2. **What Satan did to Job is scary. What do you think? (choose one)**

   - ❏ There is no such thing as Satan.
   - ❏ I don't have to worry too much about Satan.
   - ❏ I should be watching out for Satan but not afraid.
   - ❏ I should be scared to death of Satan.

3. **Check the sentence that makes the most sense to you.**

   - ❏ God never allows bad things to happen to Christians.
   - ❏ God sometimes allows bad things to happen to Christians.
   - ❏ God often allows bad things to happen to Christians.

4. **Job knew that God is perfect, holy, and just, and would never sin. He was sad to hear that he lost his children and his stuff but continued to worship God. How do you relate to the following statement?** *I can act like Job when bad things happen.*

   - ❏ Always   ❏ Mostly   ❏ Mostly not   ❏ Never

   At this, Job got up and tore his robe and shaved his head. Then he fell to the ground in worship and said: "Naked I came from my mother's womb, and naked I will depart. The LORD gave and the LORD has taken away; may the name of the LORD be praised." In all this, Job did not sin by charging God with wrongdoing. (Job 1:20-22)

5. **Mia rolled over and smacked the alarm clock.** *Another day,* **thought Mia sarcastically,** *yippee!* **Mia wasn't sure she could face another day of middle school. It all sounded so exciting when the new school year started a few weeks ago, but now kids were calling her names. She might be a little overweight, but that didn't mean that kids had the right to call her names. Why did it always have to be so hard?**

   Why do you think God allows bad things to happen in the world?

READ OUT LOUD

The book of Job can be tough to read with all its suffering, bad advice from friends, and distorted views of God. The book begins with a description of Job's character. He was a great guy who loved and respected God and hated evil. He was caught off-guard by the loss of his wealth and family. Read the story found in Job 1:1-22.

ASK

When were you caught off-guard?

DISCUSS, BY THE NUMBERS

1. There are some silly examples (carry a 10-pound Bible to school; never talk to non-Christians my age, etc.) and some in-the-middle examples (wear T-shirts with Christian slogans; pray out loud in the cafeteria during lunch; display a Christian bumper sticker on the family car, etc.). Then there are serious examples (e.g., do the best I possibly can with my homework; treat my teachers with respect; recycle; befriend the unlovely; avoid spreading rumors, etc.).

2. Here is your opportunity to lead a faith conversation on the reality of the evil one. Read 1 Peter 5:8-9 out loud to get that conversation going.

   Be alert and of sober mind. Your enemy the devil prowls around like a roaring lion looking for someone to devour. Resist him, standing firm in the faith, because you know that the family of believers throughout the world is undergoing the same kind of sufferings. (1 Peter 5:8-9)

3. Some Christians believe God protects them from evil—until something bad happens to them. Then their faith is challenged because what they believed wasn't true. Bad things happen to both Christians and non-Christians alike. Sometimes bad things happen to us because of our sin. There are consequences for wrong actions. Also bad things happen to us because of others' sin. We live in a fallen world scarred by sin.

4. Read Job 1:20-22 out loud. Ask your group members to talk about how they are like Job and unlike Job. God's sovereignty (existing outside of all things and above all things and knowing all things) is sometimes confusing to youth (and adults as well). In the case of Job, God knew what was best for him. We don't understand this fully, and neither did Job, but we can lean into Jesus, trusting that he will make all things right.

   At this, Job got up and tore his robe and shaved his head. Then he fell to the ground in worship and said: "Naked I came from my mother's womb, and naked I will depart. The LORD gave and the LORD has taken away; may the name of the LORD be praised." In all this, Job did not sin by charging God with wrongdoing. (Job 1:20-22)

5. Use this true-to-life situation to discuss bad things that have happened to your group members and their friends.

THE CLOSE

Like Job we will face trials that we won't understand this side of heaven. We are not God, although we sometimes act as though we are—or at least that we would like to be. God is so much bigger than us that we can't always fathom why God does what he does. It's like we're three-year-olds with wise grandparents: We think we understand things until something odd happens . . . and then our grandparents take care of it because they know what's best for us in ways we can't possibly comprehend. Bad things will happen to us, and like Job we can choose to say, "The Lord gives and the Lord takes away—blessed be the name of the Lord!"

With Friends Like These...

Your buddies may fail you—
so put your trust in the Lord

1. Eliphaz accused Job of not practicing the advice he gave to others when they suffered. What do you think—yes or no?

___ Do you encourage your friends when they are suffering?
___ When you suffer, do you practice the advice you've given friends who've suffered?
___ Do you trust in God to do what's right when you suffer?

But now trouble comes to you, and you are discouraged; it strikes you, and you are dismayed. (Job 4:5)

2. According to Eliphaz, you get what you deserve.

❏ I strongly agree. ❏ I agree. ❏ I'm not sure. ❏ I disagree. ❏ I strongly disagree.

3. Do you agree or disagree with this statement?

God won't give me more problems than I can handle. ❏ Agree ❏ Disagree

4. Zophar accused Job of having a shallow understanding of God. How well do you think you know God?

❏ Really well ❏ Not well enough ❏ Not at all

5. All three of Job's friends seemed to have difficulty listening to Job without first judging him and his relationship with God. Why do you think friends can be so judgmental? Why do friends sometimes want to tell you what they think you should do instead of simply listening to you? How could you be a better listener?

6. Jessica and Amy had been friends since the second grade. They were almost like sisters. Now they're in seventh grade, and they still did everything together. They had sleepovers, birthday parties, and talked for hours. They always ate lunch together—but not today. On this day Amy is sitting at another table with a new group of girls, and no one invited Jessica to sit with them. Are Amy and Jessica no longer best friends?

Why do you think friends let you down? How have you let friends down? Why do you think Christ can be trusted to never let you down?

READ OUT LOUD

In the time of Job, it was thought that people suffered because of their sin or their parents' sin. Wealth and prosperity indicated a righteous life while suffering was the result of a sinful life. Along comes the man Job—a devout God-follower . . . who lost everything. How could this be? Job's friends wanted to support him, but all of them viewed his suffering as the result of Job's sin. He needed only to repent, they said, and his wealth would be restored. While some of what Job's friends said contained parts of the truth, these three friends ultimately failed Job. Read the story out loud—the friend Eliphaz is found in Job 4:1-9; Bildad is found in Job 8:1-7; Zophar is from Job 11:1-6.

ASK

Have you ever failed as a friend?

DISCUSS, BY THE NUMBERS

1. Read Job 4:5 (below) out loud. Job encouraged and helped many people who suffered, but when it was his turn to suffer, according to Eliphaz, Job didn't practice what he had counseled others to do. For each of the three questions, ask your group members how they answered. Then ask, "Why do you think it's so easy to tell someone else how to live their lives but fail to live that way yourself?"

> But now trouble comes to you,
> and you are discouraged;
> it strikes you,
> and you are dismayed. (Job 4:5)

2. Eliphaz wrongly asserted that Job was being punished by God because of sin. While the Bible does teach that there are consequences for our actions (see Galatians 6:7-8 below), Job's sin had nothing to do with his suffering. Eliphaz had a distorted view of God and God's purposes. Job wasn't "getting what he deserved." Rather God allowed Job to be tested. Talk about a biblical picture of the awesome God who created the universe and allows things to happen to us for our own growth and to further God's kingdom.

> Do not be deceived: God cannot be mocked. A man reaps what he sows. Whoever sows to please their flesh, from the flesh will reap destruction; whoever sows to please the Spirit, from the Spirit will reap eternal life. (Galatians 6:7-8)

3. Bildad assumed Job was guilty of a colossal sin, as were Job's children. Likewise many Christians today make faulty assumptions—even crediting the Bible! For instance, *"God won't give you more problems than you can handle."* Wrong! The Bible teaches that God won't let you be tempted beyond what you can handle (see 1 Corinthians 10:13). God *will* give you more problems than you can handle. Why? So you'll learn to turn problems over to God. This is just one way we learn to trust in Christ.

4. Discuss how you and your group members need to continue learning about God as well as knowing God through experiencing his goodness and grace every day.

5. Use these questions to discuss how we so easily judge others without understanding what others are going through. Ask, "How is judging friends an encouragement?" "How is judging your friends loving your neighbor?"

6. Use this true-to-life situation to discuss actual friendship situations your group members have experienced, and how they can be better friends as they learn that ultimately they must trust Christ for their friendships.

THE CLOSE

Friendships are great. They are also important. We need them. But even though our friends try to be there for us, they will fail us at times. We still need to trust in Christ and God's plan for us even though we, like Job, can't see always see it.

1. **What is the scariest storm you've ever experienced?**

☐ Tornado ☐ Wind or dust storm
☐ Hurricane ☐ Snowstorm
☐ Rainstorm ☐ Ice or hailstorm

2. **What was it about the storm that scared you the most?**

☐ It was so much bigger than I could handle.
☐ I couldn't hide from it.
☐ I couldn't run from it.
☐ Grownups couldn't protect me.
☐ I thought I might die.

3. **I forget God's awesomeness when . . .**

☐ my life is great.
☐ I'm focused on being cool.
☐ I'm thinking about my achievements.
☐ life is miserable.
☐ I'm away from my church.

4. **What do you think about each of the following statements? T (true) or F (false)**

___ We can know as much as God.
___ Science will discover that God doesn't exist.
___ God is whatever you think God is.
___ God was around in Bible times but not today.
___ Belief in God is a crutch for people who can't face life.

5. **It isn't right that Job didn't get an answer from God as to why all the bad things happened to him.**

☐ I strongly agree. ☐ I agree. ☐ I'm not sure. ☐ I disagree. ☐ I strongly disagree.

6. *Okay*, thought Kurt. *I don't get it. I've been praying and praying, and I still don't know what I'm supposed to do about my mom and dad. They'll be divorced by this summer if they keep fighting like this. I thought if I prayed hard enough God would listen and get them to stop fighting. It's not working, though—they're fighting more than ever. Why doesn't God do something? I don't want my parents to get a divorce.*

Why do you think God isn't doing what Kurt wants?

READ OUT LOUD

Having lost nearly everything, Job questioned God about his miserable situation. Job loved the Lord and longed for answers to his misery. His friends provided Job with their faulty reasoning for his appalling condition. Then God answered Job through a storm. God revealed Job's ignorance regarding his horrible position by pointing out God's awesome power through examples found in creation. Read the story found in Job 38:1-21.

ASK

What details do you know about the beginning of the universe?

DISCUSS, BY THE NUMBERS

1. Find out if anyone in your group has been through a tornado, hurricane, rainstorm, wind or dust storm, snowstorm, or ice or hailstorm.

2. Use this item to discuss together what Job must have felt when God came to him through a storm. God revealed a small piece of his awesome power to a terrified Job. Perhaps Job thought God was about to kill him! Allow your group members to share their scary storm stories with the group to set the stage for understanding how Job must have felt when God came to him in the storm.

3. God is as awesome now as he was during the time of Job. Yet often in our technological world we get distracted from God's impressive and unmatched power. Take a few minutes to discuss what gets in the way of your group members considering God's awesomeness. Ask, "When do you most experience God's awesomeness? When do you least experience it?"

4. Each of the statements presumes we know as much or more than God. Job learned the lesson that God is God and doesn't owe him an explanation.

   • We can know as much as God. **This perspective of God says, "I know what's best, so God must do what I say—or else." If God doesn't meet one's expectations, that person puts faith on a shelf and forgets about God.**

   • Science will discover that God doesn't really exist. **While the scientific method can help us learn more about God's creation, science can't disprove God's existence. God exists outside of our realm. If anything, science will continue to show the grand design of the universe and thus the need for a Grand Designer. It's arrogant and conceited for atheists to say with certainty that there is no God.**

   • God is whatever you think God is. **To think we can create our own version of God means we believe in a very small god.**

   • God was around in Bible times but not today. **God is the same yesterday, today, and tomorrow. While there is constant change around us (the result of sin), God is perfect, and God's perfection never changes.**

   • Belief in God is a crutch for people who can't face life. **Here again is a perspective of a small god that exists as a crutch for broken people—but "strong" people don't need this "crutch." Guess what? We're *all* broken and desperately need God.**

5. In our own ignorance of the awesome power of the creator of the universe, we somehow believe that God owed Job an explanation—and owes us one as well. But God is God and can do whatever God wants. God is not mischievous or evil. God doesn't play games with our lives. God is perfect and holy and wants the best for his creation. That is why we must trust in his goodness, understanding that bad things come from sin—not from God.

6. See what answers your group members arrive at after having your faith conversations in items #1 through #5.

THE CLOSE

When we realize that God is God, we understand that God doesn't have to give us an answer—and that God loves us deeply and that we must rely completely on Jesus Christ.

Forced to Worship

Make up your mind to worship only the Lord

1. Finish this sentence:

    Two things in my life that I often put before my relationship with God are—

2. Choose TWO of the following that would help you spend five minutes each day with God.

   ☐ Say a prayer in my head three times each day.
   ☐ Pick a devotional book to read each day.
   ☐ Read a Bible passage before I go to bed each evening.
   ☐ Tell God five things I'm thankful for each day.
   ☐ Ask God at least one question each day.
   ☐ Thank God for five things each day.
   ☐ Pray for an immediate family member, an extended family member, someone at my school or on my sports team, a church member, and a friend each day.
   ☐ Pray before each meal or snack.

3. Shadrach, Meshach, and Abednego each loved God so much that they trusted him with their lives, no matter what God chose to do. What is stopping you from this kind of trust in and devotion to God?

   ☐ My non-Christian friends who make fun of me for loving Jesus.
   ☐ My non-Christian family members who don't want me to be a Christian.
   ☐ I have trouble giving up control of my life.
   ☐ I have trouble obeying a God I can't see.
   ☐ I don't have time to have that kind of relationship with Jesus.
   ☐ Other: _____

4. We should spend time with God only when we need his help.

   ☐ Strongly agree.   ☐ Agree.   ☐ Disagree.   ☐ Strongly disagree.

5. Give your opinion of the statement below—Y (yes), N (no), MS (maybe so).

   ___ If you asked my friends, they would tell you I'm a Christian.
   ___ I don't spend enough alone time with God.
   ___ Other things in life are more important to me than my relationship with God.
   ___ Today I spent more time texting than I did praying.
   ___ Reading the Bible is an important way to learn more about the God I love.

6. Cory often spent time with a boy who lived down the street. His name was Deepak. Deepak's family was Hindu. Deepak often talked about his religion, which called him and his family to worship many gods. Deepak had shown Cory pictures in his home of some of the gods. Cory thought they looked scary. They also had an "altar" where they placed offerings to the gods each day to get their attention or to ask for favors. It sounded like a lot of work to worship all these different gods. Perhaps the work was worth it, though. Cory thought he would give the Hindu gods a try. What could it hurt?

    What do you think of Cory's choice?

READ OUT LOUD

Babylonian King Nebuchadnezzar (Babylon is present-day Iraq) had a huge image built that he commanded all in his kingdom to fall down and worship. Those who refused were to be thrown into a furnace and burned to death (a common practice in Babylonian times). Three God-followers—Shadrach, Meshach, and Abednego—refused. So they were thrown into the fiery furnace where they would die a torturous, painful death. Read the story found in Daniel 3:1-30.

ASK

Why do you suppose Christians are tortured and punished by death in some countries today?

DISCUSS, BY THE NUMBERS

1. There are so many things that we often put before Christ—technology, TV, shopping, our looks, celebrities, popularity, alcohol or marijuana, friendships, sports. Discuss the reasons why it's so easy to put other things before our relationship with Christ.

2. Just like the people in today's story who chose to worship something other than God, we make daily decisions about what or who receives our attention and devotion. For example, spending some time playing video games each day is all right. However, if you spend hours playing each day—and that's all you think about or want to do—then that activity begins to take the place of your relationship with Jesus. Discuss how you and your group members can increase time spent with God and decrease time spent on God distractions.

3. Shadrach, Meshach, and Abednego all trusted in God and believed he was the only one worthy of worship, whether God chose to save them or not. Discuss how we are often silent before others about Jesus because saying something might hurt our reputations or make us look silly. Ask, "Why do you believe we're silent about Christ in a country like the United States or Canada where we can freely worship and talk about Jesus?"

4. Coming to God only when we need stuff puts God at the fringes of our lives instead of the center. With God on the outside, we won't grow closer to

Jesus and experience a full life. If we worship other things, we might falsely believe that those other things can give us salvation apart from Christ. God knew that we would be easily deceived and thus commanded that we worship only him. God is the only one worthy of our worship. Anything else is a cheap and empty imitation that never fulfills us.

5. See commentary in bold after each statement:

   - If you asked my friends, they would tell you I'm a Christian. **One measure of our devotion to God is how many of our friends know that we are Christ-followers.**
   - I don't spend enough alone time with God. **Explore why your group members (and you) may not be spending enough time with God.**
   - Other things in life are more important to me than my relationship with God. **Your group members will disagree with this statement but sometimes live as though it's true.**
   - Today I spent more time texting than I did praying. **Talk about how a prayer is like texting God.**
   - Reading the Bible is an important way to learn more about the God I love. **Yes, but often neglected.**

6. Use this true-to-life situation to talk about how worshiping other gods can hurt us—whether those gods are video games or Hindu gods.

THE CLOSE

Just as in the days of King Nebuchadnezzar, we each have a choice regarding whom or what we worship. We also can choose to worship the triune God of the Bible. God hardwired (or created) us to worship him but does not force us to do so. Given that choice some will worship themselves (e.g., their looks, abilities, wealth); others will worship stuff. And some will worship false gods that don't exist. Everybody eventually gets around to worshiping someone or something—the choice is yours. Jesus Christ invites you to repent of your sins and worship him!

1. You decide!

A drunken King Belshazzar honored God by drinking wine from God's temple cup.

❏ Yes.   ❏ Maybe.   ❏ No.

A Disembodied Hand Writes on a Wall

There are consequences for our actions

2. The world can be a scary place. King Belshazzar, who was not a God-follower, found this out when he saw the hand write on the wall. Daniel, a God-follower, wasn't afraid at all. What do you think? Christians are able to handle their fears differently than those who don't follow Christ.

❏ Always
❏ Most of the time
❏ Sometimes
❏ Hardly ever
❏ Never

3. King Belshazzar's astrologers and mediums (people who say they communicate with the dead) couldn't interpret the handwriting on the wall. God wants us to stay away from astrology and other occult practices such as communicating with the dead and witchcraft.

❏ I agree.   ❏ I disagree.   ❏ I'm not sure.

4. King Belshazzar had the perfect example in his own family of how God works in our lives—all he had to do was look to his father, King Nebuchadnezzar. But instead Belshazzar chose to reject the true God of the Bible. Why do you suppose people today, who see how Jesus works in the lives of Christians around them, still reject him as Lord and Savior?

❏ It's just not that cool of a thing to do.
❏ They don't want to give up control of their lives.
❏ They want more proof.
❏ Friends might think they're weird.
❏ They will have to change their morals.
❏ It's too much work.
❏ They'll think about it later.

5. Ben stared at the test. He'd been staring at it for the last 10 minutes. He couldn't find one question he could answer. He should have studied! It always seemed like such a waste of time—until Ben got the test. Then he wished he could go back and do it all again. Why did he let this keep happening? Ben's teacher told him that he was in danger of failing if he didn't "apply" himself. Apparently applying himself meant Ben actually needed to listen in class and do homework. What would it take for Ben to get off his butt and study?

Why do you think the consequences don't seem to motivate Ben to study?

READ OUT LOUD

King Belshazzar was in control of his kingdom, right? That's what kings usually believe. But Daniel knew differently. Daniel knew that the God of the Bible controlled the universe. God, even in silence, even when everything seems to be going wrong, is still in control. Belshazzar thought he could disrespect God and skirt past consequences. Read the story found in Daniel 5:1-31.

ASK

What are you in control of while you're at home? Bedroom? Who you text? What you eat for snacks? What?

DISCUSS, BY THE NUMBERS

1. No way! A drunk King Belshazzar disrespected God when he drank more wine from the cups stolen from the temple in Jerusalem. Whether you are young or old, drinking too much carries sometimes severe, costly consequences. The Bible commands us to not get drunk (Ephesians 5:18); it doesn't outlaw drinking. Some people choose not to drink alcohol because of the risk of alcoholism or how it will appear to non-Christians. Either way, underage drinking is against the law and therefore not okay. Plus, most underage drinking is binge drinking which is dangerous and harmful.

2. The Bible says we need not worry about providing for ourselves, that God is the one responsible for taking care of us (Matthew 6:25). We are told to give our anxieties to Christ because he truly cares for us (1 Peter 5:7). God wants us to come to him in prayer with our worries (Philippians 4:6). This is easier said than done and takes practice and encouragement from others, but it's the best way to live.

3. The world of the occult is to be avoided because it's the realm of Satan. When practiced, these activities give control to something or someone other than God—a very dangerous transfer of power. The following are occult practices:
   • Astrology
   • Fortunetelling
   • Tarot card interpretation
   • Palm reading
   • Communicating with the dead
   • Levitation games
   • Witchcraft

4. Use this opportunity to discuss what a devoted God-follower like Daniel looks like. Daniel stands in sharp contrast to King Belshazzar. Ask, "What are the qualities of a Jesus-follower?"

5. This true-to-life situation can help get a faith conversation going about how consequences teach us—they're how we learn from our sins. Some people must experience more severe consequences than others before they choose to change. Ask, "How severe must consequences become for you to change a wrong behavior?"

THE CLOSE

King Belshazzar had the benefit of a father who had to experience severe consequences before he turned to the Lord. For some reason Belshazzar chose to not learn from his father's mistakes, nor did he choose to follow God. Unfortunately Belshazzar's consequence for sinful living was death. We can choose to learn from Belshazzar's example and the examples of those around us—it doesn't have to take severe consequences for us to turn to God in repentance and learn to not repeat sinful behavior. Thank God for Jesus. In him we can experience his merciful forgiveness.

Daniel in the Lions' Den

Is your life in the pits?

1. **We all got into trouble as little kids. How did you react when you realized you were in trouble?**

   ❏ Tried to act cute and get out of it.
   ❏ Pretended my sibling did it.
   ❏ Cried.
   ❏ Tried to hide it.
   ❏ Told someone right away.
   ❏ Learned my lesson and never did it again.

2. **Daniel trusted God with his fate, no matter what God chose to do. What would your life look like if you trusted in God like this?**

   ❏ I would stress out less, knowing God is in control.
   ❏ My friends would make fun of me.
   ❏ It wouldn't be easy, but I could try to trust God one day at a time.
   ❏ I could never trust God that much.
   ❏ I would worry less about my future.
   ❏ I wouldn't care so much about what others thought of me because I would know God is in control.

3. **I bow my head and pray before a meal even when I'm with my friends or in the cafeteria at school.**

   ❏ Always　　❏ Mostly　　❏ Sometimes　　❏ Never

4. **What's one way you can learn to place your trust in God, especially during the hard times?**

   ❏ In the morning, pray for the strength to trust God today.
   ❏ Read Bible passages that display God's faithfulness.
   ❏ Talk with older Christians, asking them how they trusted God during tough times.
   ❏ Ask God to give you situations where you need to trust him so that you'll learn how.
   ❏ Before you react to a situation, think about how God would want you to react rather than how you would normally react.

5. **Finish this sentence:**

   This Bible story would be different if Daniel had not trusted in God because—

6. **The fighting had been bad enough. Tony's parents just couldn't be in the same room without screaming at each other. Tony hated it, but it was worse after they got a divorce. Now Tony saw his dad only one weekend a month. His mom cried all the time and mostly just lay on the couch and watched TV when she got home from work. Tony didn't think it could get much worse. Then today his mother told him they would have to sell their house, and he would have to go to another school. But Tony was wrong—it *could* get worse.**

   Where do you think Jesus is in relation to Tony's situation?

READ OUT LOUD

Daniel was a prophet who lived in Babylon (present-day Iraq). The Jews were conquered and taken from their Palestine homeland. The Babylonians were then conquered by the Medo-Persian Empire. Daniel found himself under the rule of King Darius, a Mede. Daniel was promoted to prime minister under Darius. Daniel, a dedicated God-follower and foreigner, was resented by the other leaders under Darius. They vowed to find something wrong with Daniel so Darius would get rid of him. Read the story found in Daniel 6:1-28.

ASK

Have you ever been wrongly accused?

DISCUSS, BY THE NUMBERS

1. We often got ourselves in trouble when we were younger. As we get older we find our lives in the pits through no fault of our own, just like Daniel. Use this activity to talk about the difficult situations your group members may face (e.g., parents' divorce, problems at school, friend problems, family conflict, etc.).

2. First, talk about what your life would look like if you were to rely more on Jesus Christ; then look at the lives of the members of your group to see how they would be different. Ask, "What is the payoff for trusting in Christ?"

3. Daniel could have secretly prayed to God for help while publicly praying to Darius. Talk about similar situations for us—not bowing your head and praying in the cafeteria before lunch; keeping quiet when others make fun of prayer.

4. Share about how you reacted to stressful life situations when you were your group members' ages. Talk about what you've learned since about relying on the Lord. Ask, "How can we move from our normal stress reactions to trusting God completely?"

5. The story would be different because Daniel most likely would've kept his God-directed prayers secret and prayed publicly to Darius, avoiding the lions' pit—but he wouldn't have been a witness to Darius nor would Daniel have encouraged his fellow God-followers. It would have been a tragedy.

6. Use this true-to-life situation to look at real situations your group members face. Talk about where Jesus is in their situations. Christ promised his presence. He promised the Holy Spirit as our helper. He promised that we can give all of our stress to him. This is easier said than done. This is why we come together as a church—to encourage, comfort, love, and learn from each other.

THE CLOSE

Christ guaranteed that we, as believers, will face problems. Like Daniel, we'll encounter situations that we won't know how to handle. And like Daniel, we can ask God for help. We can turn over worries and troubles to Christ, who promises (see John 16:33) that we can take heart because he has overcome the problems this world will throw at us.

> *"I have told you these things, so that in me you may have peace. In this world you will have trouble. But take heart! I have overcome the world." (John 16:33)*

Jonah on the Run

Christ always reaches out to us,
even when we try to hide from him

1. **Which of the three statements best describes you?**

   ❑ I'm a lot like Jonah.
   ❑ Half the time I'm like Jonah, and half the time
      I'm not like Jonah.
   ❑ I'm not too often like Jonah.

2. **Check the box after each statement that best describes your experience:**

	ALWAYS	MOSTLY	SOMETIMES	NEVER
I don't like God telling me what to do.	❑	❑	❑	❑
I don't know what God wants me to do.	❑	❑	❑	❑
I don't care about what God wants me to do.	❑	❑	❑	❑
I don't think God ever tells me to do anything.	❑	❑	❑	❑
Nobody I know listens to what God says.	❑	❑	❑	❑

3. **All eyes were on Seth. All the students in his science class—as well as his teacher—were looking at him. In the middle of a discussion on evolution, one of his friends said that since Seth was a Christian, he didn't believe evolution was true.**
   Great, just great, he thought. *Now everyone is going to think I'm a weirdo. Maybe I can just avoid the question.*
   "I go to church sometimes," Seth said. "But I don't really agree with a lot of stuff that they say."

   What do you think of Seth's response?

4. **Do you think Jonah expected he would drown when he was thrown overboard?** ❑ Yes ❑ No

   Do you think Jonah was surprised when God rescued him with a big fish instead of letting him drown? ❑ Yes ❑ No

   Do you think Jonah was happy that God rescued him? ❑ Yes ❑ No

5. **Justin was the last player picked for a team—again. This time it was for the geography map challenge in his social studies class. The teacher picked three team captains, and they picked kids they thought would help win the challenge. This alone wouldn't be such a big deal, but Justin was always picked last, no matter what the activity, at school and at church.**
   I'm not a bad guy, thought Justin. *Why don't people like me? I'm not even going to try anymore.*

   What can Justin do about his problem?

READ OUT LOUD

God gave Jonah a specific task: Tell the citizens of Israel's enemy to repent of their sins. Knowing that God would forgive them, Jonah took off in the *opposite direction*. He quickly found himself in trouble for his blatant disobedience. Read the story out loud from Jonah 1:1-17.

ASK

Who tried to get you into trouble when you were in elementary school?

DISCUSS, BY THE NUMBERS

1. Use this activity to talk about when your group members are like and unlike Jonah. Ask, "What best describes us when we act like Jonah and disobey the Lord?" "What best describes us when we obey the Lord?"

2. See commentary in bold after each statement:
   - I don't like God telling me what to do. **Offer an example from your own life so that your group members can see how easy it is for us to "not like it when God tells me what to do." For example: "I don't want to hear Jesus tell me through the Bible to love my enemy."**
   - I don't know what God wants me to do. **Agreement with this statement is an honest response regarding where many young people see themselves. Talk about the things we know for certain that God wants us to do— love God and neighbor, treat others the way we want to be treated, keep the Ten Commandments, etc.**
   - I don't care about what God wants me to do. **God gives us a choice. Do we care about God's opinion? If so, how will this affect our decisions?**
   - I don't think God ever tells me to do anything. **God has a claim on our lives. God is our creator. Christ died for our sins. The Holy Spirit lives in us. God is in the business of telling us what to do—for our own good.**
   - Nobody I know listens to what God says. **This statement gives you a chance to talk about your group members' friends who don't listen to what God says. Ask, "How should we relate to those friends?"**

3. You need not focus your attention on the pros and cons of evolution. Instead use this true-to-life situation to talk about how you can take awkward situations and turn them into opportunities to be bold for Jesus. Explore all of the options Seth had. Then discuss which ones would be the best witness for Jesus. Ask, "Could Seth believe in evolution and turn this awkward situation into an opportunity to share Christ? If so, how? If not, why not?"

4. Often people conclude that the big fish swallowing Jonah was God's punishment. Not at all! If God wished to punish Jonah, God could have let Jonah drown. The fish was God's rescue operation as well as God disciplining Jonah for his disobedience. God was there for Jonah when he needed to be disciplined, like a parent is there for a child. Jesus is there for us, too, when we need help . . . and when we need disciplining.

5. Use this true-to-life situation to discuss God's availability to us, even during the storms in our lives. Point out that God is there for us when we find ourselves discouraged and hopeless. We need not hesitate to call on God for help.

THE CLOSE

We look at Jonah's run from God and think, "How silly!" As ridiculous as Jonah's dash to avoid obeying God seems to us today, we often do the same thing! We believe we can hide our sins from Jesus. We believe we can ignore Christ, and he'll go away. We believe we can leave Christ at the church building and do whatever we want during the week. Fortunately for us, Jesus accepts us where we are in life— but refuses to leave us there. There is no escaping his love and mercy . . . or his discipline.

1. Danny caught himself. He was about to lie to his mom. Danny had been lying since he was a little kid. It usually seemed much easier than telling the truth. Lately, though, he found it hard to keep up with his lies; maybe it was because he was getting older, or the lies had gotten bigger. His mom usually knew when he was lying, and she would get really upset. Danny promised his mom again and again that he wouldn't lie—but he kept lying anyway.

50. Jonah 3:1-10
Jonah Heads to Ninevah
It's never too late to turn your life around

> How is Danny like Jonah?
> How are you like Danny?

2. If I were God I would have—

❑ sunk the ship Jonah was in, drowning all aboard—including Jonah.
❑ spared the ship and the lives of the sailors but allowed Jonah to drown.
❑ rescued Jonah with the big fish but not given him a second chance to go to Nineveh—instead I would've sent another prophet, like Amos.
❑ given Jonah as many chances as he needed.

3. God enjoys giving second chances.

❑ Strongly agree.   ❑ Agree.   ❑ Disagree.   ❑ Strongly disagree.

4. Check the box after each statement that best describes you.

	ALWAYS	MOSTLY	SOMETIMES	NEVER
I believe Christ died for my sins.	❑	❑	❑	❑
I can't seem to forgive others' sins.	❑	❑	❑	❑
I feel guilty when I sin.	❑	❑	❑	❑
I don't deserve God's second chances.	❑	❑	❑	❑
I have a tough time forgiving myself.	❑	❑	❑	❑

5. It's never too late to start obeying God, no matter how you've sinned in the past.

❑ Totally agree
❑ Mostly agree
❑ Somewhat agree
❑ Not sure
❑ Disagree

From *More Middle School TalkSheets, Epic Old Testament Stories* by David Lynn. Permission to reproduce this page granted only for use in buyer's youth group. Copyright © 2012 by Youth Specialties. www.youthspecialties.com

READ OUT LOUD

The story of Jonah is a story of a God who would rather die than spend eternity without those whom he loves. The story of Jonah is also a story of the tragedy of sin and its consequences. Fortunately this story of evil has a happy, do-over ending. Nineveh was located in modern-day Iraq. The depravity of the people of Nineveh ("fish slappers" for *Veggie Tales* fans) had reached so low that God was ready to destroy their city. Read the story of God's second chance from Jonah 3:1-10.

ASK

What do you like most about do-overs?

DISCUSS, BY THE NUMBERS

1. Like Jonah, Danny knew what the Lord wanted him to do—tell the truth. Yet he was reluctant to stop his lying even though it got him into trouble. His mother and God had given him numerous do-overs or second chances, just as Jonah had received a do-over from God. Use this activity to explore with your group members the extent of their stubbornness to obey the Lord. Ask, "Why are we often reluctant to follow God's will even though it's best for us?"

2. Talk about the characters in the book of Jonah who received second chances—Jonah, who initially runs from God; the residents of Nineveh, who were living in sin; and the sailors, whose lives were spared by throwing Jonah overboard. Ask, "Why do we often *not* give grace to others when we want God's mercy for ourselves?" Look at a few Bible characters who received do-overs from God—Moses, who murdered an Egyptian and fled, and whom God chose to return to Egypt; Samson, who was given multiple chances until his death, was used by God again and again; King David, who had an affair with Bathsheba and murdered her husband, was loved by God; Peter, who denied he knew Jesus three times in a row, was forgiven and went on to lead the early church. Finally, discuss together the Bible figures your group members have chosen.

3. We can never use up second chances from God. Yes, there are often consequences for our sins—sometimes severe ones. Yet our Lord overflows with grace as he molds us to be more like Jesus Christ. Likewise God calls us to forgive others 70 times 7—really an infinite number—because that's God's character toward us. God is always there to offer second chances. God's second chances are the central theme of the book of Jonah. God stands ready to give each of us a second chance when we repent of our sins.

4. See commentary in bold after each statement:
   - I believe Christ died for my sins. **If you don't believe Christ died for your sins, then you can't accept second chances. The death and resurrection of Christ are the keys to do-overs from God. For some people, atheism or agnosticism stands in the way of accepting God's second chances. Others simply push God, forgiveness, and spiritual matters out of their lives. If you don't think about your sins, you don't have to do anything about them . . . right?**
   - I can't seem to forgive others' sins. **Remind your group that Jesus, telling us the Lord's Prayer, says we're required to forgive others as God forgives us. We can tie our forgiveness into forgiving others to help us practice this important truth.**
   - I feel guilty when I sin. **Guilt helps you take responsibility for the wrong you've done. In this sense guilt is a good thing.**
   - I don't deserve God's second chances. **You're right; you don't deserve it. No human does anything or *is* anything that moves God toward concluding that "this person is just and righteous—I will give this person a second chance." Rather God loves us while we are sinners—and gives us second chances anyway! And nothing we've done or will do can separate us from God's love, which is made complete in the life and death and resurrection of Jesus. Don't believe you can't accept God's forgiveness—because God is ready to forgive . . . always!**
   - I have a tough time forgiving myself. **Do-overs or second chances mean we can let go of the baggage we carry from our sins. If God believes we were worth dying for, then we need to let go of the sin.**

5. We can never do something so bad that it can't get a do-over, so it's never too late to start obeying the Lord. The only unforgivable sin is not asking for forgiveness in the first place. Challenge your group members to turn to Jesus if they haven't already because he's ready to give them the free gift of salvation.

THE CLOSE

God had other plans for Jonah than drowning in an ocean storm. God gave Jonah a second chance. God stands ready to give us second chances, too. To forgive us once we repent and empower us to turn our lives around!

Jonah Gets Mad at God

We must see the world from God's point of view

1. Jonah was burning mad. He didn't get what he wanted from God. Have you ever *not* received something from God that you really wanted—and felt you deserved?

❑ Yes, many times   ❑ Yes, a few times
❑ Yes, one time   ❑ No

2. Jonah wanted the thousands of citizens of Nineveh to get what they deserved—punishment by death! Instead God was merciful and spared them. When are you most like Jonah—seeing the world from your perspective instead of God's?

❑ All the time   ❑ Most of the time   ❑ Sometimes   ❑ Hardly ever   ❑ Never

3. Do you like Jonah's description of God?

❑ Absolutely.
❑ I find it confusing.
❑ I don't believe the description is true.
❑ I never think about God, so I'm not sure.

> *He prayed to the LORD, "Isn't this what I said, LORD, when I was still at home? That is what I tried to forestall by fleeing to Tarshish. I knew that you are a gracious and compassionate God, slow to anger and abounding in love, a God who relents from sending calamity." (Jonah 4:2)*

4. What do you think? Y (yes) or N (no)

___ God's big enough to handle our temper tantrums.
___ Temper tantrums may not be the best way to communicate with God.
___ Unlike Jonah, I find it easy to love my enemies.
___ Like Jonah I find it tough to understand God's mercy.
___ I can talk with God about what angers me.

5. Christy was in the middle of telling her mom about the amazing purse she saw on a recent mall trip with her friend Chloe. It was in all the fashion magazines, and if she could get one, her friends at school would be really impressed. It cost a fortune, but really, she could use it forever, right? It had to be a quality purse to cost that much.

As she and her mom were talking, her dad came in and put the mail down on the counter. On the top of the pile was an envelope from a Christian organization that helped people in crisis. Her parents made donations to them sometimes. This envelope had a photo of a girl about Christy's age, asking to help girls caught in human trafficking. Christy couldn't stop looking at the photo. She forgot what she and her mom were talking about.

Do you think Christy will see the world from God's perspective and want to use the purse money to help stop human trafficking?

READ OUT LOUD

The last chapter of Jonah finds the prophet pouting. God refused to destroy the Ninevites, saving them instead. God's mercy extended to the Ninevites was shown to Jonah as well. God put up with Jonah's whining and teaches us a lesson about seeing the world from God's point of view. Read the story found in Jonah 4:1-11.

ASK

What does the world look like from the moon?

DISCUSS, BY THE NUMBERS

1. Jonah was *charah*—the Hebrew word which means hot or burning with anger. We are all like Jonah to some degree. That's one reason God records this story. Use this item to begin a faith conversation that compares you and your group members to Jonah. Remind your group that God is big enough for us to be mad at him. We can give our anger to God and be angry with God (knowing that, in the end, God never deserves our anger, as God is good all the time).

2. Talk together with your group about how often we look down upon others, thinking and acting as though we're superior. When we call someone "stupid" or treat someone differently because she doesn't have as much as I do, or because he's not as attractive or as athletic as I am, what are we saying about God's image that's stamped into them?

3. Read Jonah 4:2 out loud (below). Then discuss how these characteristics of God play out in our lives. Ask, "How often do you think about these characteristics of God?"
   - God's compassion and grace
   - God's patience with us—slowness to anger
   - God's abounding love
   - God's desire to not punish us

   > [Jonah] prayed to the LORD, "Isn't this what I said, LORD, when I was still at home? That is what I tried to forestall by fleeing to Tarshish. I knew that you are a gracious and compassionate God, slow to anger and abounding in love, a God who relents from sending calamity. (Jonah 4:2)

4. See commentary in bold after each statement:
   - God's big enough to handle our temper tantrums. **Often young people pick up the misperception that God can't handle our anger. Actually, God is the one who is best capable of handling our worst moods. Talk with your group members about times you have been angry with God. Ask, "Why can it be a good thing to share our true feelings with God?"**
   - Temper tantrums may not be the best way to communicate with God. **While not the best way to communicate with God—because God loves us and is good to us, all the time—we need not shy away from sharing our feelings with God.**
   - Unlike Jonah, I find it easy to love my enemies. **Jesus clearly taught that we are to love our enemies (see Matthew 5:43-44). Instead of behaving like those who don't know God, we, as followers of Christ, are to intentionally find ways to love those who hate us.**
   - Like Jonah I find it tough to understand God's mercy. **We tend to want God's mercy for ourselves but not necessarily for others.**
   - I can talk with God about what angers me. **The Apostle Paul, in Ephesians 4:26, teaches that we may express anger, as long as we do not sin in our anger. It is healthy to talk with God about what angers us so that we *don't* sin.**

5. Ask, "How would our behavior toward others change if we took God's point of view instead of our own?"

THE CLOSE

We are judgmental. We are prideful. We are self-centered. All three of these characteristics describe the human condition. Yet when we act out these characteristics, our lives don't go well. What might happen if we intentionally looked at our family members, our teachers, our friends, and yes, even our enemies, the same way that Jesus looks at them?

Missing Bible Found

Rediscovering the importance of God's Word in our lives

1. **It took King Josiah four years before he got rid of the false gods that his people worshiped. How long will it take before you are 100 percent committed to Christ?**

   ❏ I'm already 100 percent committed to Jesus.
   ❏ Another year or two
   ❏ By the end of high school
   ❏ Never

2. **The Bible wasn't important to King Josiah's grandfather or father, but it was important to Josiah. How important is the Bible in your life?**

   ❏ Incredibly important
   ❏ Sort of important
   ❏ Not that important
   ❏ A worthless collection of writings

3. **How do you suppose that the Bible, found during the reign of King Josiah, helped him do "what was right in the eyes of the Lord"? How could it help you live for Jesus? If you have a parent who is a Christian, how have you seen the Bible make a difference in her or his life?**

4. **Reading the Bible regularly can help you to—(check all that apply to you)**

   ❏ sleep at night.
   ❏ predict the future.
   ❏ love the truth.
   ❏ believe all the promises of God.
   ❏ worry less.
   ❏ know when to tell God you're sorry for your sins.
   ❏ have whiter teeth.
   ❏ develop a closer friendship with Christ.
   ❏ be more grateful.
   ❏ learn about God's awesome power.
   ❏ turn your life over to God rather than live on your own power.

5. **David's family went to see his grandma every Sunday. Usually when they got there, she was reading her Bible or had just finished reading her Bible. Basically David's grandmother was always reading the Bible! This just seemed so boring to him. What could possibly be so interesting in the Bible that kept her reading for hours? One day David got courageous: "Grandma," he asked, "what do you find so interesting in the Bible?"**

   What do you think David's grandma said to him?

READ OUT LOUD

After King David's son, Solomon, died, the Kingdom of Israel split—Israel in the North and Judah in the South. King Josiah's reign over Judah began at the young age of eight. Most likely his rule was guided by his mother and other adults at first, but he lived to rule Judah for 31 years. King Manasseh, Josiah's grandfather, did really gross, detestable, evil stuff (2 Kings 21:1-2). So did his son, King Amon (2 Kings 21:19-20), who was Josiah's father. At age 16, King Josiah began to follow the Lord (2 Chronicles 34:3). The Bible of the time (the book of the Law—at least Deuteronomy) was misplaced and forgotten by the people during the time of both King Manasseh and King Amon. The Bible was found during King Josiah's reign. Read about Josiah in 2 Kings 22:1-13.

ASK

What is your favorite time of day to read?

DISCUSS, BY THE NUMBERS

1. Read 2 Chronicles 34:3 out loud. Josiah began to follow God when he was 16. Four years later he rid his kingdom of idols. Ask, "Why is our commitment to Christ often a long-term process of spiritual ups and downs?" Explore with your group members where each of them are in relation to their commitment to Christ.

   In the eighth year of his reign, while he was still young, he began to seek the God of his father David. In his twelfth year he began to purge Judah and Jerusalem of high places, Asherah poles and idols. (2 Chronicles 34:3)

2. Use this item to discuss together why the Bible ought to be important in our lives. Ask, "How are the lives of Christ-followers different when the Bible is important to them?" "Can you be a Christ-follower and not treat the Bible as important?"

3. Read 2 Kings 22:2 out loud. Tell a story from your life about how the Bible has kept you on the right path in life. Ask your group members to tell stories about how the Bible has helped them do "what was right in the eyes of the Lord." Ask also for stories of how your group members have seen the Bible make a difference in their parents' lives. (The point is to show how living out Bible principles can make a dramatic difference in the lives of those who follow Christ.)

   He did what was right in the eyes of the LORD and followed completely the ways of his father David, not turning aside to the right or to the left. (2 Kings 22:2)

4. This activity can help your group dig deeper into the benefits of reading the Bible. First, discuss together the importance of regularly reading the Bible. This could be through the use of a devotional or through participation in a small group Bible study. Next, see which of the things your group members checked and discuss why.

5. This is an opportunity to discuss with your group why adults find the Bible helpful. Say something like, "The longer we live, the tougher life circumstances we come across. The Bible gives us God's guidance and comfort as we 'walk through the valley of the shadow of death.'"

THE CLOSE

After generations of rejecting God, Josiah took a different path. As the young king of God's people, Josiah became a God-follower and purged his nation of idols. He found the lost Bible of the day, and what God said in this document changed his life. He saw the Bible as important in his life, and it kept him and his country safe from enemies. King Josiah was one of the best kings since David. The Bible was an integral part of how he ruled. The Bible can help us, too, if we treat it as important in our lives.

High School TalkSheets, Epic Old Testament Stories

52 Ready-to-Use Discussions

David Lynn

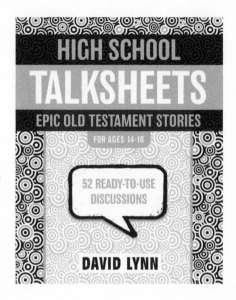

In just four short years, high school students develop friendships and habits that affect them for the rest of their lives. They need to be inspired through strong role models who embody Christian values. Where better to look for these influences than in the godly heroes of the Bible? The Talksheets series returns with another year of thought-provoking stories from the Old Testament to discuss with your youth group or bible studies. David Lynn shares discussion topics and questions written specifically with high school students in mind, promoting meaningful and thought-provoking conversations. The stories in these pages highlight pure moral principles and practices for teenagers to learn about and emulate. Each of the 52 epic Bible stories is easy to use and fit to your lesson plan, including hints and tips to facilitate conversation. These lessons also include optional activities, giving teenagers to actively participate and have fun while they learn.

Available in stores and online!

Middle School TalkSheets, Epic Old Testament Stories

52 Ready-to-Use Discussions

David Lynn

Middle school students are exposed to a lot of outside influences they don't necessarily understand. It's important to establish moral guidelines and role models early on, so they can grow with a strong understanding of Christian values. Where better to look for these role models than in the godly heroes of the Bible? The Talksheets series returns with another year of thought-provoking stories from the Old Testament to discuss with your youth group or bible studies. David Lynn shares discussion topics and questions written specifically with middle school students in mind, promoting meaningful and thought-provoking conversations. The stories in these pages highlight pure moral principles and practices for teenagers to learn about and emulate. Each of the 52 epic Bible stories is easy to use and fit to your lesson plan, including hints and tips to facilitate conversation. These lessons also include optional activities, giving teenagers the opportunity to actively participate and have fun while they learn.

Available in stores and online!

High School TalkSheets

50 Ready-to-Use Discussions on the Life of Christ

Terry Linhart

Your high school students probably think they know a lot about Jesus. But do they know how the stories of Jesus' life relate to their own? If you want to get them thinking and talking about Jesus—who he really was, and what that means for them today—you have everything you need right here.

The latest addition to the best-selling TalkSheets series, *High School TalkSheets: Life of Christ* gives you easy-to-use discussion starters and the tools to lead students into meaningful dialogue about Jesus. The one-page, reproducible handouts offer provocative questions in a compelling design that cover everything from the prediction of his birth to his ascension. Students will delve into each aspect of Jesus' life while looking at it through the lens of their own world and applying it to their own lives. These TalkSheets present every aspect of Jesus' life in a way that young teens can connect with as they learn to apply the lessons to their own lives.

TalkSheets makes the Bible relevant and engaging for students, while offering helpful hints and optional activities to help your youth ministry team effectively facilitate great conversations—without a lot of prep work.

Available in stores and online!

Middle School TalkSheets

50 Ready-to-Use Discussions on the Life of Christ

Terry Linhart

It's not hard to get middle schoolers to talk...unless you're talking about something other than the latest band, movie, or the opposite sex! If you want to get them thinking and talking about Jesus—beyond the flannelgraph, Sunday school Jesus—you have everything you need right here.

The latest addition to the best-selling TalkSheets series, *Middle School TalkSheets: Life of Christ* gives you easy-to-use discussion starters and the tools to lead students into meaningful dialogue about Jesus. The one-page, reproducible handouts offer provocative questions in a compelling design that keep in mind the unique challenges of middle school discussions. These TalkSheets present every aspect of Jesus' life in a way that young teens can connect with as they learn to apply the lessons to their own lives.

TalkSheets makes the Bible relevant and engaging for students, while offering helpful hints and optional activities to help your youth ministry team effectively facilitate great conversations—without a lot of prep work.

Available in stores and online!

High School TalkSheets on the New Testament, Epic Bible Stories

52 Ready-to-Use Discussions

David Lynn

The teenagers in your youth group love to talk about epic things—whether it's the latest blockbuster movie or a new song from their favorite band. Now you can get them talking about the epic stories found in the New Testament.

The best-selling TalkSheets series brings you an epic discussion starter in *High School TalkSheets on the New Testament, Epic Bible Stories: 52 Ready-to-Use Discussions*. The one-page, reproducible handouts are compelling and thought provoking. Not only that, they're easy for you to use: You'll find helpful hints and optional activities that can help facilitate great conversations.

Using the TalkSheets in this book, your high school students will explore and talk about epic stories like:

- Jesus' Birth
- The Teenage Jesus
- Jesus Raises a Widow's Son to Life
- Jesus Walks on Water
- Mary & Martha
- A Shriveled Fig Tree Object Lesson
- Jesus Before Pilate
- The Great Commission
- Peter & John Can't Keep Quiet
- Ananias & Sapphira Are Dead Wrong
- Barnabas, The Encourager
- Paul Before King Agrippa
- And many, many more!

Available in stores and online!

More Middle School TalkSheets on the New Testament, Epic Bible Stories

52 Ready-to-Use Discussionst

David Lynn

Every blockbuster movie with an epic story that you've seen has come back with a sequel. Think of "Star Wars" or "Lord of the Rings." Why should a TalkSheets book be any different? With the epic stories found in the New Testament, we couldn't cover it all in one edition of TalkSheets...so we're back with more!

More Middle School TalkSheets on the New Testament, Epic Bible Stories brings another year's worth of compelling and thought provoking weekly discussion starters to your middle school youth group, leading to meaningful conversations among the students in your group. Not only that, they're easy for you to use: You'll find helpful hints and optional activities that help facilitate great conversations.

With the reproducible TalkSheets in this book, you'll help your middle school students look closer at some of the epic stories of the New Testament, like:

- Jesus eats dinner with a bunch of sinners
- Peter demonstrates evangelism
- Jesus preaches for six hours
- Peter makes a jail break
- Jesus tells a story of the rich man and Lazarus
- And many more!

Available in stores and online!

ZONDERVAN®
.com

Share Your Thoughts

With the Author: Your comments will be forwarded to the author when you send them to *zauthor@zondervan.com*.

With Zondervan: Submit your review of this book by writing to *zreview@zondervan.com*.

Free Online Resources at
www.zondervan.com

Zondervan AuthorTracker: Be notified whenever your favorite authors publish new books, go on tour, or post an update about what's happening in their lives at www.zondervan.com/authortracker.

Daily Bible Verses and Devotions: Enrich your life with daily Bible verses or devotions that help you start every morning focused on God. Visit www.zondervan.com/newsletters.

Free Email Publications: Sign up for newsletters on Christian living, academic resources, church ministry, fiction, children's resources, and more. Visit www.zondervan.com/newsletters.

Zondervan Bible Search: Find and compare Bible passages in a variety of translations at www.zondervanbiblesearch.com.

Other Benefits: Register to receive online benefits like coupons and special offers, or to participate in research.

ZONDERVAN®

ZONDERVAN.com/
AUTHORTRACKER
follow your favorite authors